Assessing Advances and Challenges
in Technical Education in Brazil

A WORLD BANK STUDY

Assessing Advances and Challenges in Technical Education in Brazil

Rita Almeida, Nicole Amaral, and Fabiana de Felicio

© 2016 International Bank for Reconstruction and Development / The World Bank
1818 H Street NW, Washington DC 20433
Telephone: 202-473-1000; Internet: www.worldbank.org

Some rights reserved

1 2 3 4 18 17 16 15

World Bank Studies are published to communicate the results of the Bank's work to the development community with the least possible delay. The manuscript of this paper therefore has not been prepared in accordance with the procedures appropriate to formally edited texts.

This work is a product of the staff of The World Bank with external contributions. The findings, interpretations, and conclusions expressed in this work do not necessarily reflect the views of The World Bank, its Board of Executive Directors, or the governments they represent. The World Bank does not guarantee the accuracy of the data included in this work. The boundaries, colors, denominations, and other information shown on any map in this work do not imply any judgment on the part of The World Bank concerning the legal status of any territory or the endorsement or acceptance of such boundaries.

Nothing herein shall constitute or be considered to be a limitation upon or waiver of the privileges and immunities of The World Bank, all of which are specifically reserved.

Rights and Permissions

This work is available under the Creative Commons Attribution 3.0 IGO license (CC BY 3.0 IGO) http://creativecommons.org/licenses/by/3.0/igo. Under the Creative Commons Attribution license, you are free to copy, distribute, transmit, and adapt this work, including for commercial purposes, under the following conditions:

Attribution—Please cite the work as follows: Almeida, Rita, Nicole Amaral, and Fabiana de Felicio. 2016. *Assessing Advances and Challenges in Technical Education in Brazil*. World Bank Studies. Washington, DC: World Bank. doi:10.1596/978-1-4648-0642-1. License: Creative Commons Attribution CC BY 3.1 IGO

Translations—If you create a translation of this work, please add the following disclaimer along with the attribution: *This translation was not created by The World Bank and should not be considered an official World Bank translation. The World Bank shall not be liable for any content or error in this translation.*

Adaptations—If you create an adaptation of this work, please add the following disclaimer along with the attribution: *This is an adaptation of an original work by The World Bank. Views and opinions expressed in the adaptation are the sole responsibility of the author or authors of the adaptation and are not endorsed by The World Bank.*

Third-party content—The World Bank does not necessarily own each component of the content contained within the work. The World Bank therefore does not warrant that the use of any third-party-owned individual component or part contained in the work will not infringe on the rights of those third parties. The risk of claims resulting from such infringement rests solely with you. If you wish to re-use a component of the work, it is your responsibility to determine whether permission is needed for that re-use and to obtain permission from the copyright owner. Examples of components can include, but are not limited to, tables, figures, or images.

All queries on rights and licenses should be addressed to the Publishing and Knowledge Division, The World Bank, 1818 H Street NW, Washington, DC 20433, USA; fax: 202-522-2625; e-mail: pubrights@worldbank.org.

ISBN (paper): 978-1-4648-0642-1
ISBN (electronic): 978-1-4648-0643-8
DOI: 10.1596/978-1-4648-0642-1

Cover art: © Luis Alegre / World Bank. Further permission required for reuse.
Cover design: Debra Naylor, Naylor Design, Inc.

Library of Congress Cataloging-in-Publication Data has been requested.

Contents

Foreword ix
Acknowledgments xi
About the Authors xiii
Executive Summary xv
Abbreviations xxiii

	Introduction	1
	Note	4
	References	4
Chapter 1	General Education and the VET System in Brazil: An Overview	5
	Introduction	5
	Recent Improvements and Challenges in Education	5
	Structure of Brazil's Education System	8
	The VET Structure in Brazil in an International Context	10
	Technical Education in Brazil: VET at the Upper Secondary Level	12
	Notes	15
	References	16
Chapter 2	Selected Design Features and Implementation Arrangements of the VET System in Brazil	19
	Introduction	19
	VET Tracks and Program Modalities	19
	A Typology of Technical Courses	21
	Modes of Delivery: Classroom, Distance, and Workplace Learning	23
	Main VET Providers	24
	Eligibility Criteria: Merit, Ordering, and Priority Criteria	30
	VET Regulatory Framework: Bridging Occupations and Courses	32
	Certification of Competencies in Technical Education	33

	VET Teacher Selection, Career Trajectories, and Compensation	34
	Spending on and Funding of Technical Education	35
	Monitoring and Evaluation of Technical and Technological Education	39
	Expanding VET with the National Technical Education and Employment Program (PRONATEC)	42
	Notes	49
	References	51
Chapter 3	Brazil's VET System: Implementation Challenges, Opportunities, and International Examples	53
	Introduction	53
	Aligning Skills Provided by the VET System with the Needs of the Labor Market	53
	Monitoring and Evaluation of the VET System	58
	Disseminating Information to Help Students in Their Education and Career Choices	61
	Raising the Quality and Relevance of the VET System	66
	Promoting Innovation in VET	71
	Implications for PRONATEC: Expanding VET and Reaching the Most Vulnerable	74
	Notes	78
	References	79
Chapter 4	Policy Directions for Reform	83
	Summary	83

Boxes

I.1	World Bank Systems Approach for Better Education Results (SABER)	3
2.1	The Experience of São Paulo: Paula Souza Center	30
2.2	Expanding State-Level VET: The Experiences of São Paulo and Minas Gerais	48
3.1	Developing an Education and Training System for the Mining Sector in Chile	55
3.2	International Examples of Workplace Learning	57
3.3	Australia's National Centre for Vocational Education Research	62
3.4	Information Systems: Examples from Chile and the United States	63
3.5	Alma Laurea, Italy: Placing Emphasis on Labor Market Intermediation	64

3.6	Virginia's Academic and Career Plans of Study	66
3.7	Mexico's Occupational Competency Standardization and Certification Council (CONOCER)	68
3.8	Building a Flexible Cadre of Teachers	70
3.9	VET Teacher and Trainer Preparedness in Switzerland	71
3.10	VET for Innovation and Competitiveness: Chicago's City Colleges	73
3.11	Ideas for Innovating in VET	74

Figures

I.1	Challenges to Hiring Skilled Workers As Reported by Employers by Region and Country: Brazil, circa 2003	2
1.1	Education Quality, National Math Score Averages (IDEB and SAEB): Brazil, 2005–11	7
1.2	Number of Enrollments in Vocational Education by Administrative Dependence, 2015	11
1.3	Percentage of Upper Secondary Students Enrolled in Vocational or Prevocational Programs: Selected Countries, 2011	12
1.4	Academic and Vocational Education Tracks, Brazil	13
1.5	Enrollment by Level of Basic Education: Brazil, 2013	14
1.6	Enrollments in Technical Education at the Upper Secondary Level by Modality: Brazil, 2013	14
1.7	Percentage of Population (15 Years and Older) That Had Enrolled in Technical Education: Brazilian States, 2013	15
2.1	Vocational and Technical Education and Training (VET) Program Enrollments as Percentage of Total Enrollments in VET: Brazil, 2007	20
2.2	Industries with Highest Percentage of Vocational and Technical Education and Training (VET) Graduates by Level of VET: Brazil, 2007	22
2.3	Technical Courses with Largest Enrollments through Bolsa Formação: Brazil, 2010	22
2.4	Total Enrollment in Vocational and Technical Education and Training (VET) by Type of VET Provider: Brazil, 2007	25
2.5	Enrollment in Technical Education by Provider Type: Brazil, 2014	25
2.6	Brazil's Education Funding System since 2007, FUNDEB	36
2.7	PRONATEC: Program Beneficiaries and Providers	45
2.8	PRONATEC Funding Flow, 2011–14	47
3.1	Percentage of Students by Type of Course and Income Quintile: Brazil, 2007	76
3.2	Wage Premiums for Technical Education Graduates Relative to Those with Only Academic Upper-Secondary Education, 2007	77

Maps

2.1	Location of E-TEC Brazil Centers	24
2.2	Federal System of Vocational Education: Brazil, 2010	27

Tables

1.1	Public Spending on Education by Education Level: Brazil, 2002–13	6
1.2	International Standard Classification of Education (ISCED1997) and Brazilian Education System	9
2.1	Eligibility Criteria for Vocational Education (Secondary Level), State of São Paulo	31
2.2	Public Expenditure on Upper Secondary and Technical Education and Enrollment by State: Brazil, 2008	38
2.3	Monitoring Systems for Technical Education by Type of Provider: Brazil, 2007	42
2.4	PRONATEC Targets for Enrollment by Policy: Brazil, 2011–14	47
3.1	Categories and Types of Indicators Used in VET Evaluation, 2012	59
3.2	Secondary Education Course Loads, Total Hours per Year by Modality: Brazil, 2012	75

Foreword

Brazil is investing massively in a scale-up of vocational and technical education and training (VET) through its national flagship program, Programa Nacional de Acesso ao Ensino Técnico e Emprego (PRONATEC, National Program for Access to Technical Education and Employment). This report assesses in detail VET institutions and policies in Brazil, taking an in-depth critical view of upcoming opportunities. In doing so, it shares important international best practices on selected operational issues identified as strategic bottlenecks for the delivery of technical education, especially at the upper secondary level. It also explores multiple sources of information, including a desk review of existing reports and papers, inputs and data provided by Brazil's Ministry of Education, and interviews with multiple stakeholders and practitioners at the federal and state levels.

The report concludes with important and feasible policy implications that are urgent to incorporate in Brazil VET policy making. It highlights the need to promote both a better alignment of the supply of and demand for skills at the subnational level and a better monitoring and evaluation system, including the monitoring of student learning and of the trajectories into the labor market or into higher education. Issues of student career guidance and teacher quality also emerge as areas of strategic importance to the Brazilian VET system in the years ahead. The report concludes with specific policy recommendations for PRONATEC.

Reynaldo Fernandes, Professor, University of São Paulo

Acknowledgments

This report was drafted by Rita Almeida, senior economist, and the team lead for this study, Education Global Practice (GEDDR), World Bank; Nicole Amaral, short-term consultant, GEDDR; and Fabiana de Felicio, executive director, METAS. It benefited from outstanding contributions by Gabriel Barrientos, program assistant, GEDDR, at different stages. The contact author is Nicole Amaral (nicole.l.amaral@gmail.com).

The team is extremely grateful for the ongoing support and overall guidance provided by Reema Nayar, practice manager, GEDDR, and Magnus Lindelow, program leader, LCC5C. And the authors are very grateful to the following institutions for their valuable contributions: the Instituto de Pesquisa Econômica Aplicada (IPEA, Institute for Applied Economic Research, Serviço Nacional de Aprendizagem Industrial (SENAI, National Service of Industrial Learning)–São Paulo, Serviço Nacional de Aprendizagem Comercial (SEAC, National Commercial Training Service), Secretariat of Education of São Paulo State (Secretaria da Educação do Estado de São Paulo), Secretariat of Labor of São Paulo State (Secretaria do Trabalho do Estado de São Paulo), Centro Paula Souza (São Paulo State network of vocational and technical schools), and Fundacao Roberto Marinho (Roberto Marinho Fund) and especially to Aparecida Lacerda (Fundação Roberto Marinho), Instituto de Pesquisa e Estratégia (IPECE Institute for Research and Economic Strategy of Ceará), Secretariat of Education of Ceará, Secretariat of Social Development and Labor of Ceará, and Secretariat of Science and Technology of Ceará. The report benefited especially from discussions and preliminary presentations to Marcelo Feres and the PRONATEC team at the Secretária de Educação Profissional e Tecnológica (SETEC, Office of Vocational and Technological Education) in the Ministério da Educação (MEC, Ministry of Education). The SETEC team also provided data and presentations that served as a basis for this report.

We also thank the participants in several invited presentations and workshops held at the World Bank in Washington, DC (December 2013, June 2014, and January 2015), IPEA Brasilia (April 2013, May 2014), and Centro Paula Souza in São Paulo (November 2013). We are especially grateful to IPEA staff for their comments, including Sergei Soares (president), Paulo A. Meyer M. Nascimento, Divonzir Gusso, Miguel Nathan Foguel, and Aguinaldo Maciente. We are also thankful for the suggestions by colleagues from the World Bank, including Cristian Aedo, practice manager, GEDDR; Maria Madalena dos Santos, consultant, GEDDR; Mark Dutz, sector leader, GTCDR; Thomas Kenyon, senior private sector development specialist, GTCDR; Joana Silva, senior economist, GSPDR; Andre Loureiro, economist, GEDDR; Renata Gukovas, extended-term consultant, GPVDR; Rita Costa, consultant; Michael Drabble, senior education specialist, GEDDR; Margaret Grosh, sector manager, GSPDR; Jee-Peng Tan, consultant; and Naércio Menezes Filho (Insper and USP). Their insightful comments have substantially improved this volume.

This report functions as a background paper for the Brazil Skills and Jobs Task at the World Bank (Silva, Almeida, and Strokova 2015). That task is part of an emerging multisector program at the World Bank that supports work on skills development, employability, and productivity growth in Brazil. In particular, it aims to contribute to the government's objective of achieving more and better jobs and fostering productive inclusion.

About the Authors

Rita Almeida currently leads policy, research, and operational support in a wide set of education and skills policies in Latin America and the Caribbean. Her experience ranges from labor market analysis, skills development policies, activation and graduation policies, labor market regulations, and social protection for workers, to firm productivity and innovation policies and the evaluation of social programs. Rita has experience in managing multicultural teams in diverse areas of human development at World Bank Headquarters and Country Offices. She coauthored *The Right Skills for the Job: Rethinking Training Policies for Workers* (World Bank 2012). She has raised funding and established partnerships with foundations and think tanks for the delivery of joint analytical work, training, and dissemination events.

Her work has been published in *The Economic Journal, American Economic Journal: Applied Economics, Journal of International Economics, Labour Economics,* and *World Development*. Her research has been covered in multiple reports, including the *World Development Report* (World Bank), and by reports of the Inter-American Development Bank and the organization for Economic Co-operation and Development.

Rita holds an M.A. degree from the Portuguese Catholic University in Lisbon and a Ph.D. in economics from Universitat Pompeu Fabra. She has been an IZA fellow since 2003.

Nicole Amaral joined the Inter-American Development Bank in 2015 and is a Senior Associate in the Office of Strategic Planning and Development Effectiveness. Nicole worked for three years in the Education and ICT Global Practices at the World Bank as a Junior Professional Associate and Consultant. She has focused on skills development policies and TVET and human capital for innovation, and she has worked in operations in Brazil, Chile, and Colombia. Prior to coming to the World Bank, Nicole worked on early education programs as a contractor for the U.S. Department of Health and Human Services, as well as in entrepreneurship and innovation promotion as a Princeton in Latin America fellow at Endeavor in Santiago, Chile. Nicole holds an M.A. in Latin American studies, with a concentration in political economy, from Georgetown University.

Fabiana de Felicio is a consultant in research and social policy evaluation. She has worked with the Instituto Unibanco, Instituto Votorantim, World Bank, UNESCO, and the Education Ministry. She served as Director of the Educational Research Directory until 2008.

Fabiana was a core team member in the development of new indicators measuring the quality of education at the subnational level for basic and higher education institutions. She also participated in studies identifying good practices in schools and municipal systems jointly with UNICEF and the World Bank, in addition to studies focused on the Brazilian education funding system (Fundef and Fundeb).

She holds an M.A. degree in economics from São Paulo University.

Executive Summary

Introduction

Despite the impressive progress in education coverage over the last decades, Brazil continues to experience important obstacles to achieving higher completion rates at the secondary level and, generally, to improving the quality of its education system. From 1980 to 2010, the enrollment of students aged 7–14 years steadily increased, from 80.9 percent to 96.7 percent, and during that period the largest investments in education were made. However, despite Brazil's standing as one of the world's largest economies, much of its labor force continues to be low-skilled. The average schooling in Brazil is only 8.4 years, corresponding to the completion of only a lower secondary education. In fact, no segment of Brazil's education system crystallizes the quality gap with the Organisation for Economic Co-operation and Development (OECD) and East Asian countries as clearly as secondary school (see Bruns, Evans, and Luque 2012). A high percentage of secondary students are enrolled in night classes, which deliver only four hours of instruction a day, compared with seven hours or more in most OECD countries and even longer school days in the leading East Asian countries. Infrastructure is also lacking, as schools lack the libraries, science labs, and computer and language facilities that most OECD students enjoy. The curricula are overloaded and largely oriented toward memorization, and almost every state secondary school system faces a severe shortage of qualified math and science teachers (Bruns, Evans, and Luque 2012).

Within this context, vocational and technical education and training (VET) has emerged as an option that offers quicker student integration into the workforce and more directly meets the needs of the labor market. This sharper focus on VET is based on several factors. First, VET captures learning in a diverse set of applied vocations and may be a good way of keeping at-risk and unmotivated youth in school through the upper secondary level. Second, although tertiary education is expanding in coverage, the progress has not been fast enough. Tertiary education is also not necessarily the best way to absorb all the students interested in acquiring additional qualifications. Third, VET programs are one possible way to adapt a low or unskilled labor force and prepare workers for new opportunities in new or fast-growing sectors. Finally, there is also some evidence that part of the productivity challenge in Brazil is related to the skills currently available in the workforce or the lack thereof—for example, see Almeida and Jesus Filho (2011) for evidence on the amount of time needed to fill a job vacancy.

The Programa Nacional de Acesso ao Ensino Técnico e Emprego (PRONATEC, National Program for Access to Technical Education and Employment), a federal program created in 2011 and coordinated by the Ministério da Educação (MEC, Ministry of Education), is aimed at expanding the supply of VET students. PRONATEC serves as an umbrella to coordinate a variety of existing and new vocational education and training policies, including both ensino técnico or cursos técnicos (TEC, technical education) and cursos formação inicial e continuada (FICs, initial and continuing training courses). Under this program, MEC has established partnerships with other ministries (social development, tourism, and communication, among others) to identify and select potential trainees for technical courses. Initially, PRONATEC was developed with a plan to invest R$24 billion (approximately US$10.8 billion) between 2011 and 2014 with a target of almost 8 million enrollments: 2.4 million in TEC education and 5.6 million in FIC training courses. Figures from 2014 put current enrollments under PRONATEC at approximately 7.2 million, meaning the program is close to achieving its target. Although MEC finances these programs, PRONATEC is executed at the subnational level, by local municipalities, states, or through Sistema S, the federal network of VET institutions. PRONATEC also intends to expand the VET programs and courses it finances to provision by the private sector.

Goals and Findings of This Report

This report maps institutions and policies in vocational and technical education and training in Brazil and assesses recent advances and challenges in their delivery. The report is based on interviews with clients and stakeholders, including MEC-SETEC (Secretaria de Educação Profissional e Tecnológica—Office of Vocational and Technological Education), and a review of secondary materials. The report has two main goals. First, it seeks to lay out Brazil's system of VET, describing the policies and institutions involved in its delivery, but with a special focus on the upper secondary level (cursos técnicos de nível médio, hereafter simply technical education).[1] Second, it seeks to identify challenges constraining the effective delivery of VET and suggests relevant international good practices for overcoming selected issues. It concludes with specific recommendations for the implementation of PRONATEC. This report also complements three companion papers that examine (1) enrollments in technical and vocational education over time (Almeida et al. 2015); (2) the returns of VET in Brazil (Almeida, Anazawa, and Menezes Filho 2014); and (3) a mapping of shorter training programs, typically aimed at the most vulnerable (Gukovas et al. 2013).

To date, there is only anecdotal evidence of skills gaps or mismatches in Brazil. Consequently, in the medium run policy makers should give priority to building a high-quality general education system. Although there is some evidence that employers are not fully meeting their needs with the skills available in the workforce, much more research is needed to understand the depth and breadth of this issue. As a result, policy makers should first and foremost invest in improving the quality of general education, which sets the foundation of knowledge and the base on which technical education students build.

Over the past decade, secondary and postsecondary technical education in Brazil has experienced important growth. From 2007 to 2011, enrollment in technical education grew by 60 percent, from 780,000 to 1.25 million students. Nevertheless, in 2011 technical education represented only 13.5 percent of the total enrollment at the upper secondary level, reaching approximately 8 million students.[2] This number is still considerably lower than the levels of enrollment in technical education in countries such as France, Germany, Portugal, and Spain, where enrollment in technical education accounts for about 40 percent of the total number of students enrolled at the upper secondary level.

This report reveals that the delivery of VET in Brazil includes a combination of short- and longer-term courses offered in multiple modalities and through a variety of providers. The overall VET system in Brazil is divided into three categories: (1) cursos tecnológicos (technological education) at the tertiary level; (2) ensino técnico or TEC (technical education) at the upper secondary level; and (3) FICs, which are short-term training courses not directly linked to a specific level of education. Technical education can be delivered either alongside the general secondary academic track (concomitante and integrado), or it can be offered following the completion of the general upper secondary education (subsequente). Short-duration technical courses (FICs) usually target low-skilled individuals who are already outside of the formal education track. VET in Brazil is provided in both a classroom format and as distance learning, and some courses also provide on-the-job (or workplace) learning and training through apprenticeships (estágios).[3] Whether an apprenticeship is a required part of the program, however, is at the discretion of the provider as well as dependent on the availability of local apprenticeship opportunities.

Private providers play a prominent role in the provision of short-term (FIC) courses, whereas public schools at the federal and state levels are more important providers of technical courses at the upper secondary level. The main providers of VET in Brazil include Sistema S, the Brazilian Federal Network of Education Institutes (Institutos Federais, Federal Institutes), and the state-level networks of upper secondary education. Private schools are also an important player, especially for the provision of FIC courses. Although the Lei de Diretrizes e Bases (which outlines the responsibilities for the provision of education) gives the states the primary responsibility for providing VET at the secondary level, municipal-level schools also provide some VET. Nevertheless, they have the smallest share of enrollment. Providers at all of these levels offer both FIC and TEC programs.

Recommendations

Looking ahead, this report identifies five strategic policy areas that should be strengthened for more efficient delivery of technical education in Brazil.

First, promote a closer alignment of the supply of VET courses with the quantity and quality of the skills demanded by the labor market and with student preferences. This is a challenge in many regions, because of the diversity of labor market needs at the subnational level and even the large diversity within states. The report argues that to address this challenge, Brazil should consider innovative governance arrangements within a sector approach. One example is the use of skills councils or similar skills ecosystems. At the state level, VET providers could invite local representatives from different sectors of the economy (for example, industry, commerce, tourism, services) to present their stances on what types of occupations and professionals are in the greatest demand. These inputs from local representatives could be complemented by quantitative and qualitative information on the placement rates of students from different types of VET programs. Programs that more easily place students in jobs, especially high-quality jobs, should be further supported and see their number of vacancies expanded. Fostering this coordination is especially important because the completion of most VET programs should require that students complete an on-the-job training/learning component through apprenticeships or other workplace learning arrangements. In addition, early evidence suggests that employers increasingly demand socioemotional skills (including persistence and self-control), which workplace learning often helps to strengthen. Apparently, few VET programs place an emphasis on these types of skills.

Second, improve the monitoring and evaluation system, especially regarding the quality and relevance of VET for the labor market. To date, and in spite of the quality of the data available, Brazil continues to lack a solid monitoring and evaluation system that (1) tracks provider quality or course performance, (2) includes objective measures of student knowledge (captured by nationwide standardized tests), and (3) includes students' transition rates to tertiary education or to the labor market. Through the Sistema Nacional de Informações da Educação Profissional e Tecnológica (SISTEC, National Information System for Professional and Technological Education), MEC tracks a range of socioeconomic characteristics for all students who have completed or are completing technical courses at the upper secondary level.[4] However, SISTEC does not systematically cover all FIC students (only when these students take FIC courses in institutions that also offer technical courses) and does not track students into higher education or into the labor market. In addition, although general secondary education has a modern system of student assessment (Ferrão et al. 2001), national examinations such as the Exame Nacional do Ensino Médio (ENEM) are not compulsory for all students completing an upper secondary education, regardless of their track.[5] As a consequence, there is no way of evaluating learning and the quality of technical schools. In addition, few federal- or state-level technical schools use the insertion of students into the labor market as a way to measure performance and to systematically guide and inform policy implementation based on this information.

Third, develop a strategic career guidance framework based on a solid information system to help guide students and their families when making educational and career decisions. Such interventions are critical to helping reverse the stigma that is persistently associated with technical education. A lack of general career counseling is an important gap in the system at the upper secondary level. International experience shows that such counseling helps students develop their professional interests and focus their attention on the differences between career paths and rates of return. However, developing a framework for career guidance, which would include qualified career guidance professionals and up-to-date information systems as portals for students and their families, rests on ensuring that a strong and systematic system of monitoring and evaluation is in place to provide reliable and timely data for these needs.

Fourth, improve the quality and relevance of VET through better-prepared teachers. The quality challenge is strongly linked to the difficulties in hiring and retaining highly qualified teachers with a command of the latest technical knowledge in their field. Although the quality of VET teachers in the Federal Institutes and Sistema S is generally considered good, public sector hiring policies still leave few opportunities for teachers to move easily between teaching and other occupations in their field. This permeability across academia and the labor market is of critical importance to keeping VET curricula current and relevant to the labor market. This situation has already become a binding constraint in many states, especially in the most remote areas where it is difficult to recruit teachers. It is also a constraint in adding, dropping, or modifying the existing VET programs because the specialized skills evolve, and yet teachers spend little time in industry. Hiring new teachers and reallocating the existing teachers where needed can be difficult. At the same time, the lack of job security and benefits packages facing private sector VET teachers—which does not attract the strongest candidates—leaves the quality of VET provision in private institutions uneven, if not lacking. This report argues that the adoption of more flexible contracts that allow teachers to be well trained for teaching but also obtain sectoral experience is critical, especially in the public network. The latter can be achieved by ensuring that trainers in VET institutions spend some of their time working and by promoting more flexible pathways of recruitment that also allow those with sectoral experience to be part of VET institutions. Some states such as Ceará have already experimented with a middle ground between the two extremes, finding ways to attract and maintain high-quality VET teachers, while at the same time allowing for the flexibility needed to evolve technical programs as necessary. Finally, improving quality and relevance may not necessarily imply building a full national qualifications framework for Brazil—a country with a high level of diversity and, in many parts of the country, relatively low administrative capacity. Nevertheless, improving quality and consistency across different levels and VET qualifications requires a better and more standardized organization of the competencies, qualifications, and occupations requiring vocational and technical skills.

Fifth, promote innovation in technical education through innovative pedagogies and low-cost infrastructure. Based on OECD experience, this report suggests two interventions to help the VET system become more innovative. On the one hand, refocusing VET pedagogies on solving real-world challenges presented by firms is one way of ensuring that students are applying their learning in a way that will be required in the workplace. This approach may also help to address the lack of apprenticeship opportunities available to all VET students. Case study and project-based learning can also be complemented by student competitions in which students compete to solve the challenges presented by different sectors using the knowledge and skills being developed in the classroom. On the other hand, technical education must incorporate the latest technology and offer a set of physical tools that students can use in applying their learning in new and innovative ways. Although supplying every VET institution with the infrastructure and technology available in different economic sectors would be both costly and unrealistic (especially in the more remote regions of Brazil), innovative models of relatively low-cost, multipurpose, and yet high-tech laboratories (such as the Fab Labs model developed at the Massachusetts Institute of Technology) might be one way to give students the tools they need to innovate both inside and outside the classroom.

Because Brazil is investing in a rapid scale-up of its VET programs through PRONATEC, this report concludes with specific policy recommendations for this effort. First, it stresses the importance of capitalizing on opportunities for further research, especially in conducting rigorous impact evaluations to assess the cost-effectiveness of many of the interventions that are part of this program and the most effective ways of delivering them. Such an approach has already been applied to several other policy questions in Brazil.[6] Meanwhile, at least two very important and general questions are of critical importance for the successful implementation of VET policies and of PRONATEC. The first concerns the evidence on labor market returns to technical education (career-wise—wages, progression) via the general secondary education track. The second concerns second-generation questions on how these programs should be delivered on the ground. How effective are on-the-job components versus more academic learning? How important is it to complement cognitive learning with noncognitive skills for different age groups? How effective is a system of career guidance in promoting the integration of students into the labor market? Among these questions, for two particular policies—both promoted under PRONATEC—there may be room for impact evaluations based on an initial pilot. The first is an evaluation of the cost-effectiveness of distance learning for VET students (also known as E-TEC Brasil) in producing high-quality graduates who have skills relevant to the labor market. Distance learning is especially relevant to the poorest states and the most remote locations where it is challenging to recruit high-quality teachers and to provide students with more diverse VET programs where the local job market for certain skills is not strong. The second is an evaluation of Bolsa Formação, a program targeting low-income students and low-skilled workers that finances TEC courses for students in the public network and FIC courses for beneficiaries of unemployment insurance or of other social assistance programs.[7] It is important to understand how effective scholarships have been in actually placing students in educational and career opportunities.

In a second phase, PRONATEC should carefully assess whether and how it has had an impact on the target beneficiaries, including the most vulnerable in the country. According to research by Almeida et al. (2015), historically graduates of technical education programs tend to be socioeconomically better off than students in the academic upper secondary track. It is important to consider how best to expand technical education to reach the less advantaged, including rethinking contents and the heavier-than-average course loads that currently characterize technical education compared with the academic track. In addition, it is critical that more and better data and studies are produced to support the expansion of PRONATEC, particularly for certain delivery modes for which little evidence is available so far (for example, online learning).

Notes

1. This report focuses more specifically on vocation and technical education and training as it is integrated into the formal education system in Brazil at the secondary and tertiary levels. A companion paper (Gukovas et al. 2013) examines in greater depth the different active labor market policies (ALMPs) in Brazil, including the short-term training provided outside the formal schooling system.
2. Instituto Nacional de Estudos e Pesquisas (INEP, National Institute of Studies and Research) and MEC; Censo Escolar (School Census), 2007 and 2011.
3. The majority of the technical courses have a mandatory apprenticeship period, but this requirement is generally left to the discretion of the course provider. The workload for the apprenticeship is not included in the total hours defined in the National Catalogue of Technical Courses (Catálogo Nacional de Cursos Técnicos).
4. SISTEC is an administrative data set that includes for all students information about the courses they are taking (including name of the course, technological area, workload, type of provider—public, private, Sistema S, regional location) and about the students (including name, identification, status of the enrollment—active, inactive, or completed course—and whether the student receives a scholarship).
5. ENEM is a national exam that measures general secondary education subjects such as math and Portuguese.
6. The World Bank has supported or led multiple efforts in Brazil, including the recent evaluations of Pernambuco's Teacher Bonus Program by Bruns and Ferraz (2012) and the World Bank–supported evaluation of Rio de Janeiro's Creches programs on child and family outcomes, "Free Access to Child Care, Labor Supply, and Child Development", by Attanasio et al. (2014).
7. Bolsa Formação offers professional and technological education. It has two modes: Bolsa Formação offers initial and continuing courses (short courses of 160 class hours or more) to beneficiaries of unemployment insurance and productive inclusion

programs of the federal government; Bolsa Formação Estudante offers technical courses (of longer duration, at least 800 classroom hours) to students in the public networks.

References

Almeida, Rita, Leandro Anazawa, and Naercio Menezes Filho. 2014. "Ministério Do Trabalho e Emprego, Brasil, e pelo Banco Mundial." World Bank, Washington, DC.

Almeida, Rita Kullberg, Leandro Anazawa, Naercio Menezes Filho, and Ligia Maria De Vasconcellos. 2015. "Investing in Technical & Vocational Education and Training: Does It Yield Large Economic Returns in Brazil/" Policy Research Working Paper no. WPS 7246, World Bank Group, Washington, DC. http://documents.worldbank.org/curated/en/2015/04/24411547/investing-technical-vocational-education-training-yield-large-economic-returns-brazil.

Almeida, Rita, and Jaime Jesus Filho. 2011. "Demand for Skills and the Degree of Mismatches: Evidence from Job Vacancies in the Developing World." Unpublished manuscript, World Bank, Washington, DC.

Attanasio, Orazio, Ricardo Paes de Barros, Pedro Carneiro, David Evans, L. Lima, Pedro Olinto, and Norbert Schady. 2014. "Free Access to Child Care, Labor Supply, and Child Development." Unpublished Working Paper, Centre for the Evaluation of Development Policies at the Institute for Fiscal Studies.

Bruns, Barbara, David Evans, and Javier Luque. 2012. *Achieving World-Class Education in Brazil: The Next Agenda*. Washington, DC: World Bank.

Bruns, Barbara, and Claudio Ferraz. 2012. *Paying Teachers to Perform: The Impact of Bonus Pay in Pernambuco*. Brazil: Society for Research on Educational Effectiveness.

Ferrão, M. E., K. Beltrão, C. Fernandes, D. Santos, M. Suarez, and A. Andrade. 2001. "O SAEB—Sistema Nacional de Avaliação da Educação Básica: Objetivos, características e contribuições na investigação da escola eficaz." *Revista Brasileira de Estudos de População* 18 (1/2): 111–30.

Gukovas, Renata, Joana Silva, Karla Carolina Marra, and Jociany Monteiro Luz. 2013. "Qualificações e empregos políticas ativas e passivas de mercado de trabalho no Brasil: Estrutura, inovações e oportunidades." Ministry of Labor and Employment, Rio de Janeiro, and World Bank, Washington, DC.

Abbreviations

ACP	academic and career plan
ALMP	active labor market policy
BNDES	Banco Nacional de Desenvolvimento Econômico e Social (Brazilian Development Bank)
CBA	Center for Bits and Atoms
CBO	Classificação Básica de Ocupações (Basic Classification of Occupations)
C2C	Career to College (Chicago)
CCC	City Colleges of Chicago
CEE	Conselho Estadual de Educação (State Board of Education)
CEFET	Federal Center of Technological Education
CENTEC	Centro de Educação Tecnológica (Center for Technological Education)
CERTIFIC	Certificação Profissional e Formação Inicial e Continuada (Initial Training and Professional Certification and Continuation)
CIEE	Centro de Integracao Empresa-Escola (Center for Work-School Integration)
CNC	Confederação Nacional do Comércio de Bens, Serviços e Turismo (National Confederation of Trade in Goods, Services, and Tourism)
CNE	Conselho Nacional de Educação (National Board of Education)
CNI	Confederação Nacional da Indústria (National Confederation of Industry)
CONOCER	Occupational Competency Standardization and Certification Council (Mexico)
CVT	Centro Vocacionais Tecnológicos (Technological Vocational Centers)
CVTECS	Centros Vocacionais Técnicos (Technical Vocational Centers)
EFT	European Training Foundation
EJA	educação jovens e adultos (youth and adult education)

EMI	ensino médio integrado (integrated secondary education)
ENEM	Exame Nacional do Ensino Médio (National High School Exam)
FAT	Fundo de Apoio Trabalhador (Fund for Worker Support)
FICs	cursos de formação inicial e continuada (initial and continuing training courses)
FIES	Fundo de Financiamento ao Estudante do Ensino Superior (Fund for Financing Higher Education for Students)
FIES-TEC	Fundo de Financiamento ao Estudante do Ensino Técnico (Fund for Financing Technical Education for Students)
FNDE	Fundo Nacional de Desenvolvimento da Educação
FUNDEB	Fundo de Manutenção e Desenvolvimento da Educação Básica e de Valorização dos Profissionais da Educação (Fund for the Maintenance and Development of Basic Education and Enhancement of Education Professionals)
IBGE	Instituto Brasileiro de Geografia e Estatística (Brazilian Institute of Geography and Statistics)
IDEB	Índice de Desenvolvimento da Educação Básica (Basic Education Performance Index)
IFSP	Instituto Federal de São Paulo (São Paulo Federal Institute)
INCRA	Instituto Nacional de Colonização e Reforma Agrária (National Institute of Colonization and Agrarian Reform)
INEP	Instituto Nacional de Estudos e Pesquisas (National Institute of Studies and Research)
ISCED	International Standard Classification of Education
ISCO	International Statistical Classification of Occupations
LBD	Lei de Diretrizes e Bases da Educação Nacional (Law of National Guidelines for Education)
LSAY	Longitudinal Surveys of Australian Youth
M&E	monitoring and evaluation
MDS	Ministério do Desenvolvimento Social e Combate à Fome (Ministry of Social Development and Fight against Hunger)
MEC	Ministério da Educação (Ministry of Education)
MinTur	Ministério de Turismo (Ministry of Tourism)
MIUR	Ministry of Education, University and Research
MTE	Ministério do Trabalho e Emprego (Ministry of Labor and Employment)
NCVER	National Centre for Vocational Education Research (Australia)
NGO	nongovernmental organization

NQF	national qualifications framework
OECD	Organisation for Economic Co-operation and Development
PISA	Programme for International Student Assessment (OECD)
PNAD	Pesquisa Nacional por Amostra de Domicílios (Household Sample National Survey)
PNL	Projeto de Lei do Plano Nacional de Educação (Project Law of the National Education Plan)
PRONATEC	Programa Nacional de Acesso ao Ensino Técnico e Emprego (National Program for Access to Technical Education and Employment)
PROUNI	Programa Universidade para Todos (University Program for All)
RAIS	Relação Anual de Informações Sociais (Annual Social Information)
SABER	Systems Approach for Better Education Results (World Bank)
SAEB	Sistema de Avaliação da Educação Básica (Basic Education Evaluation System)
SEBRAE	Serviço Brasileiro de Apoio às Micro e Pequenas Empresas (Brazilian Support Service for Micro and Small Enterprises)
SEE	Secretaria de Estado da Educação de São Paulo (São Paulo State Secretary of Education)
SENAC	Serviço Nacional de Aprendizagem Comercial (National Commercial Training Service)
SENAI	Serviço Nacional de Aprendizagem Industrial (National Service of Industrial Learning)
SENAR	Serviço Nacional de Aprendizagem Rural (National Rural Education Service)
SENAT	Serviço Nacional de Aprendizagem do Transporte (National Transportation Learning Service)
SESC	Serviço Social do Comércio (Social Service of Commerce)
SESCOOP	Serviço Nacional de Aprendizagem do Cooperativismo (National Service for Cooperative Learning)
SEST	Serviço Social do Transporte (Transportation Social Service)
SETEC	Secretaria de Educação Profissional e Tecnológica (Office of Vocational and Technological Education)
SIOPE	Sistema de Informações sobre Orçamentos Públicos em Educação (Information System on Public Budgets in Education)
SISTEC	Sistema Nacional de Informações da Educação Profissional e Tecnológica (National System of Professional and Technological Education)

SISTEMA S	Conjunto de entidades ligadas à indústria (SESI e SENAI), ao comércio (SESC e SENAC), ao transporte (SEST e SENAT), à agricultura (SENAR), às cooperativas (SESCOOP) e às micro e pequenas empresas (SEBRAE)—set of entities related to industry (SESI and SENAI), trade (SESC and SENAC), transportation (SEST and SENAT), agriculture (SENAR), cooperatives (SESCOOP), and micro and small enterprises (SEBRAE)
SMEs	small and medium enterprises
TEC	ensino técnico (technical education)
VET	vocational and technical education and training
WFD	workforce development

Introduction

Brazil's education system is a complex structure with overlapping entities, both public and private, at the federal, state, and municipal levels. Vocational and technical education and training (VET) is integrated into traditional education at the secondary and tertiary levels, and yet at the same time it is offered as separate programs by different public and private educational providers, especially for those who are already outside traditional education trajectories. As a result of the complexity of the VET system and the federal government's decision to massively scale it up, the government instituted the Programa Nacional de Acesso ao Ensino Técnico e Emprego (PRONATEC, National Program for Access to Technical Education and Employment) in 2011. Coordinated by the Ministério da Educação (MEC, Ministry of Education), PRONATEC is aimed at dramatically expanding the supply of VET students and providing an umbrella for the country's overlapping VET policies.

Some observers, however, find the need for this expansion somewhat unsubstantiated—strong evidence of skills gaps or skill mismatches in Brazil is lacking. Nevertheless, even though the empirical evidence does not strongly suggest a scarcity of skilled workers, anecdotal evidence indicates that employers are not satisfied with the skills developed for the workforce (see figure I.1).[1]

More research is needed, however, to quantify and qualify this preliminary evidence in ways that can guide education policy. Consequently, short- and medium-term policy debates should focus on improving the quality of general education, which is the base on which technical education students build and which would allow for the improvement and expansion of VET.

In the context of a large scale-up under PRONATEC and the complexity of the Brazilian VET system, this report seeks to (1) present an overview of Brazil's system of vocational and technical education and training in the context of the larger Brazilian education system; (2) map the policies and institutions involved in the delivery of vocational and technical education, especially at the upper secondary level (*cursos técnicos*); and (3) identify key advances and challenges that are constraining the effective delivery of education services, particularly VET. The report also provides examples of countries overcoming some of these same challenges. Brazil could consider some of these strategies in the context of its own scale-up of VET. Overall, the report seeks to offer suggestions for improving the operationalization and implementation of the PRONATEC program on the ground.

Figure I.1 Challenges to Hiring Skilled Workers As Reported by Employers by Region and Country: Brazil, circa 2003

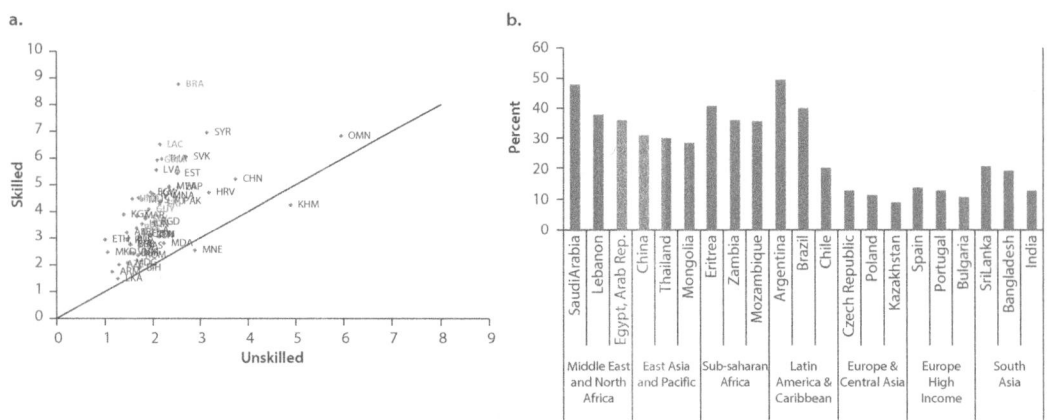

Source: Aedo and Walker 2012.
a. Average number of weeks needed to fill vacancy
b. Share of firms reporting skills as an obstacle to hiring

This report is informed by a desk review of materials collected and disseminated by the Secretaria de Educação Profissional e Tecnológica (SETEC, Office of Vocational and Technological Education) in MEC, as well as interviews with federal- and state-level partners and counterparts, including the states of São Paulo, Ceará, Piauí, and Minas Gerais. The underpinnings for this data collection exercise were loosely based on the SABER workforce development (WfD) analytical framework and a questionnaire put together by the World Bank's Education Global Practice. This report, however, does not attempt to be a full-fledged SABER WfD report. Instead, it explores several categories of SABER (see box I.1) in order to effectively collect information on multiple dimensions of the system. The analytical framework proposed by Almeida, Behrman, and Robalino (2011) underlies this work. That framework maps market failures with policy responses and highlights different market and government failures in the provision of VET. In addition, a detailed desk review was conducted of international best practices in technical education programs in relevant countries and contexts of the member countries of the Organisation for Economic Co-operation and Development (OECD).

The report is organized as follows. Chapter 1 presents an overview of the general education system in Brazil and contextualizes VET within the broader system of education in Brazil.

Chapter 2 describes the VET system in detail: the different modalities and tracks in which VET programs are offered; a typology of technical education courses; modes of delivery; the main VET providers; the specifics of each provider; eligibility criteria, the VET regulatory framework, and the certification of courses; teacher selection in VET; the financing of VET; and the existing monitoring and evaluation (M&E) system for VET, as well as the new expansion under

Box I.1 World Bank Systems Approach for Better Education Results (SABER)

The World Bank's SABER workforce development (WfD) tool is used to collect and analyze policy data on education systems around the world. It incorporates evidence-based frameworks to highlight the policies and institutions that matter most to promoting learning for all children. SABER evaluates the quality of education policies against evidence-based global standards, using new diagnostic tools and data to provide an objective snapshot of how well the policies of a country's education system are oriented toward ensuring learning. The SABER WfD tool focuses on three key functional dimensions of WfD policies and institutions:

1. Strategy—the alignment of workforce development with a country's national goals for economic and social development
2. System oversight—the governance arrangements that shape the behavior of key stakeholders involved, including individuals, employers, and training providers
3. Service delivery—the arrangements for managing the provision of services in order to achieve results on the ground.

The SABER WfD tool also identifies nine policy goals that are used as a guide for data collection in this report: (1) setting a strategic direction for WfD; (2) fostering a demand-driven approach to WfD; (3) strengthening critical coordination for implementation; (4) ensuring efficiency and equity in funding; (5) ensuring relevant and reliable standards; (6) diversifying pathways for skills acquisition; (7) enabling diversity and excellence in training provision; (8) fostering relevance in public training programs; and (9) enhancing evidence-based accountability for results.

Source: World Bank 2013.

PRONATEC. Throughout this discussion, the report focuses more specifically on technical education at the upper secondary level.

Chapter 3 identifies five strategic areas in which there is great potential for improvements for technical education in the short and medium term. Specifically, it discusses the importance of aligning technical education with the needs of the labor market; takes a closer look at the strengths and weaknesses of the monitoring and evaluation system for VET in Brazil; builds on the importance of M&E and highlights the current state of disseminating this information to students, parents, and other stakeholders and providing career guidance for students; discusses the quality and relevance of VET in Brazil, including qualifications frameworks as well as steps to improve the cadre of teachers and trainers for VET; looks at VET from the viewpoint of its potential to contribute to innovation, growth, and productivity in the country; and discusses the implications for PRONATEC, focusing particularly on considerations for reaching the most vulnerable in Brazil.

It concludes with an Index that offers policy recommendations based on the findings in the report.

Before proceeding, a note of caution is in order: one of the central challenges in the development of this report was the scarcity of data on vocational and technical education and training in Brazil. This factor is one of the main conclusions and policy recommendations of the report: the importance of systematized monitoring and evaluation and the collection of data on the quantity, quality, and results of VET. This type of information should be a key input for decision making by policy makers, VET providers, and students in the context of the large scale-up in Brazil over the next several years of VET through PRONATEC.

Note

1. Maciente and Araújo (2011) report that because of the recent expansion of higher education, the flow of new professional graduates in engineering, production, and construction will be insufficient to meet the demand for these professions if Brazil's growth exceeds 4 percent a year through 2020. Similarly, Gusso and Nascimento (2011) demonstrate that demand continues to be high because options for higher education in engineering, production, and construction are expanding faster on average than other programs.

References

Aedo, C., and I. Walker. 2012. "Is Labor Demand in LAC Accommodating to Inferior Skills?" *Skills for the 21st Century in Latin America and the Caribbean*. Washington, DC: World Bank Publications.

Almeida, Rita, Jere Behrman, and David Robalino, eds. 2011. *The Right Skills for the Job? Rethinking Training Policies for Workers*. Washington, DC: World Bank.

Gusso, D., and P. Nascimento. 2011. *Contexto e dimensionamento da formação de pessoal técnico-científico e de engenheiros*. Radar, Brasília: IPEA.

Maciente, Araújo, and T. C. Araújo. 2011. *Requerimento técnico por engenheiros no Brasil até 2020*. Radar, Brasília: IPEA.

World Bank. 2013. "SABER—Systems Approach for Better Education Results: Strengthening Education Systems to Achieve Learning for All." http://saber.worldbank.org/index.cfm.

CHAPTER 1

General Education and the VET System in Brazil: An Overview

Introduction

This chapter is an overview of the current state of education in Brazil. The aim is to contextualize the following chapters of this report, which will focus more specifically on vocational and technical education and training (VET) at the secondary level, which is known as ensino técnico in Brazil. This chapter summarizes recent improvements and current challenges in education in Brazil and describes briefly the overall structure of the education system, the structure of VET and technical education within Brazil's education system, and how it compares with the structure of technical education internationally.

Recent Improvements and Challenges in Education

The Brazilian economy is the world's eighth largest, but labor productivity remains low. Therefore, looking ahead at improving the quality of education is critical. Many economists have identified improving labor productivity and the quality of formal education and training as one of the core approaches to addressing the issue of productivity. Indeed, Brazil's education system has undergone great improvements over the past 20 years. The enrollment rates for students aged 7–14 years have steadily increased, from 80.9 percent in 1980 to 89 percent in 1991 to 98.5 percent in 2010 and as of 2012, about 88 percent of those that enrolled made it to the last grade of primary school.[1] These increases resulted in turn in a large rise in the average length of schooling, which is now at 8.4 years, corresponding to completion of a lower secondary education.

The largest investments in education in Brazil have been made over the past 10 years: public spending on education as a percentage of the gross domestic product (GDP) increased by nearly 47 percent over a period of nine years, growing from 4.5 percent of GDP in 2000 to 5.8 percent in 2010 to 6.6 percent in 2013 (table 1.1).[2] An important part of the increase in education spending has been at the secondary level. Between 2002 and 2013, public spending on lower

Table 1.1 Public Spending on Education by Education Level: Brazil, 2002–13
percentage of GDP

| | | | | Level of education | | | |
| | | | | Fundamental education | | | |
Year	All levels	Basic education	Pre-primary	Primary	Lower secondary	Upper secondary	Tertiary
2002	4.8	3.8	0.4	1.7	1.3	0.5	1.0
2003	4.6	3.7	0.4	1.5	1.2	0.6	0.9
2004	4.5	3.7	0.4	1.5	1.3	0.5	0.8
2005	4.5	3.7	0.4	1.5	1.3	0.5	0.9
2006	5.0	4.1	0.4	1.6	1.5	0.6	0.8
2007	5.2	4.3	0.4	1.6	1.5	0.7	0.9
2008	5.4	4.5	0.4	1.7	1.7	0.8	0.9
2009	5.7	4.8	0.4	1.8	1.8	0.8	0.9
2010	5.8	4.9	0.4	1.8	1.7	0.9	0.9
2011	6.1	5.0	0.5	1.8	1.7	1.1	1.0
2012	6.4	5.3	0.6	1.8	1.7	1.2	1.1
2013	6.6	5.4	0.7	1.8	1.7	1.2	1.2

Source: Instituto Nacional de Estudos e Pesquisas (INEP, National Institute of Studies and Research), 2013, http://www.inep.gov.br/.

secondary education increased from 1.3 percent of GDP to 1.7 percent. In upper secondary, spending increased from 0.5 percent to 1.7 percent of GDP during the same period. The results of this increase in spending are clear in the progress in the access to education in recent years: the average years of schooling for the 25- to 35-year-old cohort had grown to 9.3 years by 2011.

This increase in spending has been matched not only by an expansion in enrollments, but also by improvements in quality. The 2009 results for the Program for International Student Assessment (PISA), which measures secondary school student learning outcomes in more than 70 countries, confirmed Brazil's progress with a 52-point increase in math since 2000, indicating that students gained a full academic year of math mastery over the decade. The overall score increase—from 368 to 401—is the third largest on record. The most significant progress was registered between 2005 and 2013 in primary education (5th grade) where the Sistema de Avaliação da Educação Básica (SAEB, Basic Education Evaluation System) scores increased by 16 percent in math (figure 1.1). Test scores in math and Portuguese at the lower secondary level (9th grade) experienced smaller improvements during this period (4.2 percent in math). Upper secondary (11th grade) actually experienced a small decrease in scores in math of –0.7 percent.

Nevertheless, the development of a competitive workforce in Brazil over the next decade will require more than simply completion of a secondary education. On the one hand, Brazil should continue investing in expanding access to tertiary education. In 2013 only 15 percent of youth between 26 and 35 years old

Figure 1.1 Education Quality, National Math Score Averages (IDEB and SAEB): Brazil, 2005–11

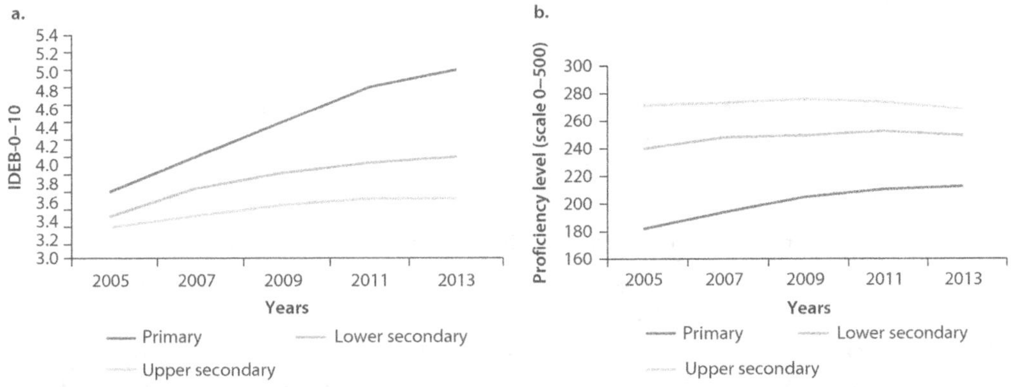

Source: IDEB/MEC 2015.
Note: National averages in SAEB test scores for Portuguese reveal a similar trend.
a. Indice de Desenvolvimento da Educação Básica (IDEB, Basic Education Development Index), score 0–10
b. Sistema de Avaliação da Educação Básica (SAEB, Basic Education Evaluation System), score 0–500

had completed a tertiary education.[3] On the other hand, it is important to provide all students with the right skills for the labor market, including at the secondary level (Almeida, Behrman, and Robalino 2011). Building a world-class secondary education system with the right skills for the twenty-first century remains an ongoing challenge (see Bruns, Evans, and Luque 2012). Meanwhile, anecdotal evidence suggests that increasingly these skills need to be cognitive and noncognitive. Moreover, empirical evidence suggests that there are diminishing returns to workers with secondary degrees. Between 1995 and 2009, those who had completed a secondary education experienced a decrease in real wages of 10 percent, while those with a higher education (but without postgraduate degrees) experienced an increase in real wages of only 3 percent (Menezes Filho 2012).

There is also evidence that the labor market in Brazil became increasingly polarized during this period. At the extreme ends of the distribution, postgraduates and unskilled workers saw the highest increase in real wages (approximately 36 percent). This polarization is consistent with a global pattern of demand for highly qualified workers with strong analytical skills and demand for unskilled labor that requires person-to-person interactions such as domestic labor (Menezes Filho 2012). Labor market data in Brazil are similarly signaling that twenty-first-century skills are important for the next generation of workers. Producing graduates with these skills will be a critical challenge for the education system over the next decade—that is, graduates with the ability to think analytically, ask critical questions, master new skills and content quickly, and operate with a high level of communication and interpersonal skills, including foreign language mastery and an ability to work effectively in teams.

At the same time, important challenges remain in trying to continue to improve the quality of general primary and secondary (including upper secondary) education, which together provide the base on which technical education students build. Bruns, Evans, and Luque (2012) identify four key challenges for the Brazilian basic education system:

- Raising teacher quality
- Protecting the early development of the most vulnerable children
- Building a world-class secondary education system
- Maximizing the impact of federal policy on basic education.

In fact, no segment of the Brazilian education system crystallizes the quality gap with the Organisation for Economic Co-operation and Development (OECD) and East Asian countries as clearly as secondary school. A high percentage of Brazil's secondary students are enrolled in night classes, which deliver only four hours of instruction a day, compared with seven or more hours of instruction in most OECD countries and even longer school days in the leading East Asian countries. In Brazil, schools lack the libraries, science labs, and computer and language facilities that most OECD students enjoy. The curricula, which are overloaded, are largely oriented toward memorization, and almost every state secondary school system faces a severe shortage of qualified math and science teachers (Bruns, Evans, and Luque 2012).

Structure of Brazil's Education System

Brazil's formal education system is divided into basic education and tertiary education. Basic education consists of nursery school (ages 0–3), preprimary (ages 4 and 5); primary (ages 6–10); lower secondary (age 11–14); and upper secondary (ages 15–17), which includes technical education.[4] Tertiary education consists of undergraduate, master, doctoral, and postdoctoral programs. These programs may or may not have a technological focus. Table 1.2 maps these levels, comparing them with United Nations Educational, Scientific, and Cultural Organization (UNESCO)'s International Standard Classification of Education (ISCED 1997).[5]

Until 2009, school was compulsory for children aged 7–14, corresponding to a primary and lower secondary education (ensino fundamental). In 2006, Brazil's constitution was amended (Emenda Constitucional No. 59) to lower the age of obligatory public education to six-year-olds and fundamental education was divided into nine grades (1st through 9th). The amendment was scheduled to take effect gradually, and in 2010 school attendance in Brazil became compulsory for ages 6–17. In 2013 Lei 12.796/13 again amended educational requirements and extended free public education to children aged 4–17 (preschool through high school as shown in table 1.2). By the end of 2015, the education system must be fully adapted and compliant with this new amendment, making school compulsory for all children aged 4–17. This age group will be the first group required to attend preschool (ages 4–6) as well as complete a primary and secondary education.

Table 1.2 International Standard Classification of Education (ISCED1997) and Brazilian Education System

Levels, ISCED 1997 (definition)	Brazilian education system (target age range)	
Does not apply to ISCED	Creche (ages 0–3, nursery education)	
ISCED 0 (from age 3, preprimary level of education)	Creche (age 3) and *pré-escola* (ages 4–5)	Basic Program (compulsory education)
ISCED 1 (primary level of education)	Ensino fundamental (1st to 5th grades, ages 6–10)	
ISCED 2 (lower secondary level of education; subcategories: 2A prepares students for continuing academic education, leading to 3A; 2B has stronger vocational focus, leading to 3B; 2C offers preparation for entering workforce)	Ensino fundamental (6th to 9th grades, ages 11–14)—2A type; 2B type is not usual.	
ISCED 3 (upper secondary level of education; subcategories: 3A prepares students for university-level education at level 5A; 3B prepares students for entry to vocationally oriented tertiary education at level 5B; 3C prepares students for workforce or for postsecondary nontertiary education at level ISCED 4)	Ensino médio (ages 15–17)—3A type Ensino médio profissionalizante: integrado and concomitante—3C type Both 3A and 3C prepare students for tertiary education (5A or 5B).	Basic Program
ISCED 4 (postsecondary nontertiary; subcategories: 4A may prepare students for entry to tertiary education, both university level and vocationally oriented; 4B typically prepares students to enter the workforce)	Ensino medio profissionalizante: subsequente (ages 18+)— 4A or 4B; could also be considered 3C.	
ISCED 5 (first stage of tertiary education; subcategories: 5A prepares students for professions with high skill requirements and includes master's degree; 5B technological courses are shorter than those of tertiary-type (minimum of two years) and focus on practical, technical, or occupational skills for direct entry into the labor market, although some theoretical foundations may be covered in the respective programs)	Cursos tecnológicos (ages 18–24, tertiary education)—5B type Cursos de graduação (ages 18–24) Mestrado and mestrado profissional (tertiary education)—5A type	Tertiary Education
ISCED 6 (second stage of tertiary education leading to an advanced research qualification— doctoral and postdoctoral degrees)	Doctorate and postdoctorate	

Source: OECD 2012.
Note: ISCED = International Standard Classification of Education; OECD = Organisation for Economic Co-operation and Development.

Because of high repetition and dropout rates, an additional modality of formal education has been designed specifically for youth and adults with low educational attainment: educação de jovens e adultos (EJA, youth and adult education).[6] In spite of progress, Brazil's education system continues to exhibit significant age-grade distortion—that is, the target age for each education level does not reflect the actual average age of the students enrolled. In 2014, 20 percent of students in primary and lower secondary education (ensino fundamental) were overage, and in upper secondary education (ensino medio) the age-grade distortion was 28.2 percent. The system also exhibits high repetition rates—that is, students failing to pass into the next grade. High repetition rates contribute in part to the high levels of age-grade distortion (8.5 percent for primary and lower secondary and 11.8 percent for upper secondary in 2013), as well as the high dropout rates (2 percent for primary and lower secondary and 8.1 percent for upper secondary in 2013).[7] These high repetition and dropout levels indicate that many Brazilians are leaving school before completing their secondary education, and often even before completing lower secondary. In 2013, about 40 percent of Brazilians ages 25–34 had not completed an upper secondary education.[8]

The VET Structure in Brazil in an International Context

Over the last few decades, many countries have increased efforts to offer more comprehensive programs for upper secondary education, including improving the curricula of the general/academic upper secondary track and reshaping vocational education. The expansion of upper secondary in OECD countries has been driven by the modernization of both academic and vocational programs, increasing demand, and efforts to universalize access to education (Bruns, Evans, and Luque 2012). A vocational upper secondary or postsecondary nontertiary education is the highest level of attainment for more than 50 percent of 25–64 year olds in Austria, the Czech Republic, Germany, Hungary, the Slovak Republic, and Slovenia (see Bruns, Evans, and Luque 2012).

Vocational education often has multiple arrangements. Although an international classification of VET programs does not yet exist, most programs exhibit the following combination of characteristics:

1. VET covers different levels of education (lower secondary, upper secondary, postsecondary nontertiary, and tertiary).
2. VET and academic programs may have a common core or may exist independently.
3. In some programs, part of the vocational education coursework is carried out in school (school-based), and the other part of the coursework may be conducted on-site through local employers (work-based). Alternatively, programs may be exclusively school-based or work-based.
4. Depending on the kind of VET program, students who finish a program may be certified as having completed a formal education level, and completion of a VET program may allow them to take courses at the next education level.
5. VET may include apprenticeship/workplace learning programs.

In some countries such as Sweden, certain subjects are common to both academic and vocational programs. Other countries such as Germany conduct vocational and general education as simultaneous programs. In Germany, one part of the program is taught in educational institutions (school-based) and is complemented by a work-based component. In other countries, such as France and Italy, vocational education is completely independent of academic programs.

In Brazil, vocational and technical education and training at the secondary level—called technical education—has a special role in improving the skill levels of the Brazilian labor force. VET is defined as the modality of education that provides students with labor market–relevant skills for a particular occupation or industry, and it is recognized by the relevant authorities in the country.[9] However, some of the challenges for vocational and technical education, especially at the secondary level, include finding the correct balance between academic and vocational content as well ensuring a smooth transition to work for secondary education graduates who do not go on to higher education. Public-private partnerships can be helpful in orienting the vocational content of the curriculum toward skills that are in demand (Bruns, Evans, and Luque 2012). Several states, such as Minas Gerais, Rio de Janeiro, São Paulo, and Ceará have spearheaded new models of VET education, but such models are not yet standard or carried out at scale throughout the country.

In Brazil, VET has experienced important growth over the last several years. From 2007 to 2014 alone, enrollment in technical education (at the secondary level) grew by 123 percent, from approximately 780,000 to 1.74 million students (figure I.1).

Nevertheless, vocational and technical education represents only 13.6 percent of total enrollments in upper secondary education in 2011 (about 8 million students) and had increased to 15.3 percent by 2013.[10] This proportion of upper secondary students enrolled in vocational or prevocational programs is one of the

Figure 1.2 Number of Enrollments in Vocational Education by Administrative Dependence, 2015

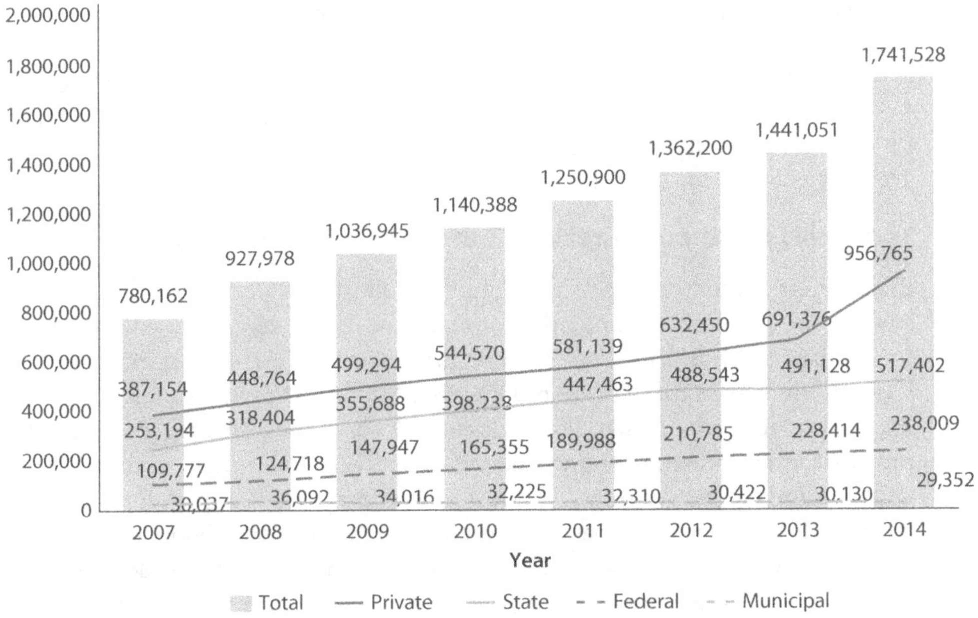

Year	Total	Private	State	Federal	Municipal
2007	780,162	387,154	253,194	109,777	30,037
2008	927,978	448,764	318,404	124,718	36,092
2009	1,036,945	499,294	355,688	147,947	34,016
2010	1,140,388	544,570	398,238	165,355	32,225
2011	1,250,900	581,139	447,463	189,988	32,310
2012	1,362,200	632,450	488,543	210,785	30,422
2013	1,441,051	691,376	491,128	228,414	30,130
2014	1,741,528	956,765	517,402	238,009	29,352

Source: MEC/INEP 2015.

Figure 1.3 Percentage of Upper Secondary Students Enrolled in Vocational or Prevocational Programs: Selected Countries, 2011

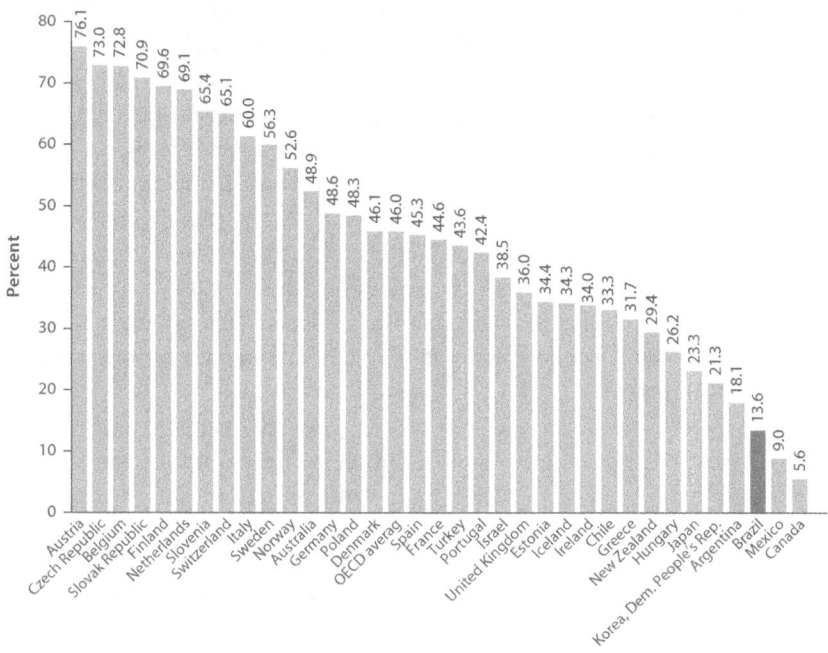

Source: OECD 2011.

smallest among OECD and G20 countries. In some countries such as France, Germany, Portugal, and Spain, enrollment in technical education is about 40 percent of enrollments in upper secondary education. In Austria, the Czech Republic, and the Slovak Republic, enrollments in technical education account for over 60 percent of total enrollments in upper secondary education. The OECD average is 46 percent (see figure 1.3).[11]

Technical Education in Brazil: VET at the Upper Secondary Level

Brazil offers several types of VET. Figure 1.4 illustrates the options available to students in Brazil after completing primary and lower secondary education. At the tertiary level, Brazil offers *technological* education. At the upper secondary level, it offers *technical* education. However, *training* courses, also known as formação inicial e continuada (FIC, initial and continuing training courses), are provided independently of any academic education level—that is, they do not require completion of primary and lower secondary. The completion of training courses (FICs) typically does not count toward the completion of a formal academic education level, and thus such courses do not qualify students to take courses at the next level (for example, moving from secondary to tertiary

Figure 1.4 Academic and Vocational Education Tracks, Brazil

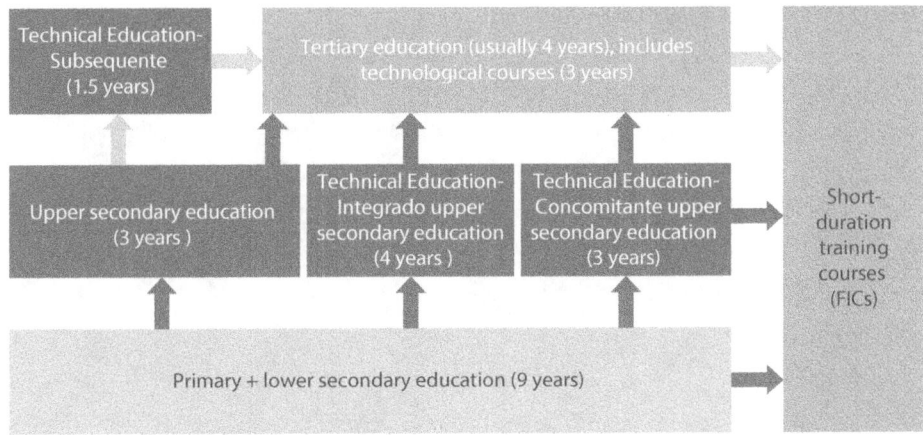

Source: Based on Lei de Diretrizes e Bases da Educação Nacional, No. 9.394, 1996.

education). In some programs such as Sistema S, students can accumulate FIC classes toward the completion of different education levels.

This report focuses primarily on VET at the secondary level, also known as technical education (ensino técnico de nível médio), which forms part of the formal schooling system in Brazil. Technical education is provided in three alternative modalities at the upper secondary level: (1) academic and vocational courses offered as one program in the same school—integrado; (2) a complementary but separate technical program for students who are completing an academic upper secondary program, which is frequently carried out in two separate schools—concomitante; and (3) a technical program for students who have already concluded an academic upper secondary program—subsequente. Figure 1.5 reports the percentage of enrollments across the different levels of education.

Figures 1.5 and 1.6 show that almost all enrollments in integrado are VET combined with an academic upper secondary education program. However, a small part of integrado is comprised of VET combined with educação jovens e adultos (EJA, youth and adult education)—a fourth modality designed specifically for youth and adults (18 years and older) who have fallen behind or who dropped out of school before completing a secondary education. The subsequente modality is undertaken after the academic secondary education is completed.

Students who enroll in and complete technical education have a slightly different profile than those in the general academic upper secondary track. According to Almeida, Anazawa, and Menezes Filho (2014) who use data from the 2007 Pesquisa Nacional por Amostra de Domicílios (PNAD,

Figure 1.5 Enrollment by Level of Basic Education: Brazil, 2013

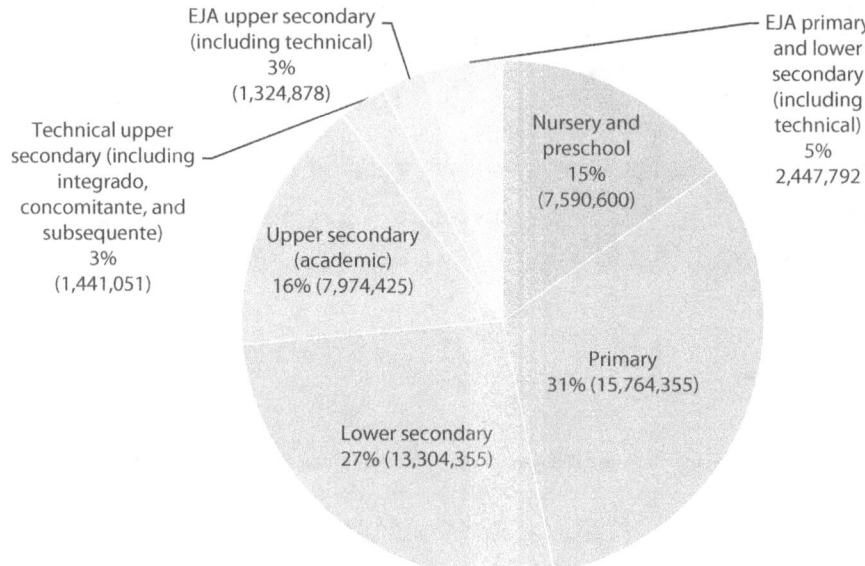

Source: Instituto Nacional de Estudos e Pesquisas (INEP, National Institute of Studies and Research) 2013, http://www.inep.gov.br/.
Note: EJA = educação jovens e adultos (youth and adult education).

Figure 1.6 Enrollments in Technical Education at the Upper Secondary Level by Modality: Brazil, 2013

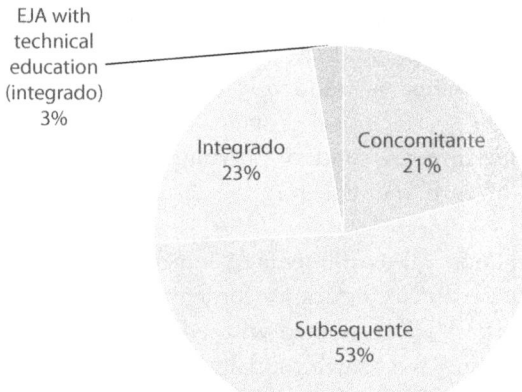

Source: Instituto Nacional de Estudos e Pesquisas (INEP, National Institute of Studies and Research), 2013, http://www.inep.gov.br/.
Note: EJA = educação jovens e adultos (youth and adult education).

Household Sample National Survey), most technical education students are from urban areas (96.4 percent), where the majority of upper secondary schools, including those that offer technical education, are located. Those who have completed a technical education track tend to be on average 35

Figure 1.7 Percentage of Population (15 Years and Older) That Had Enrolled in Technical Education: Brazilian States, 2013

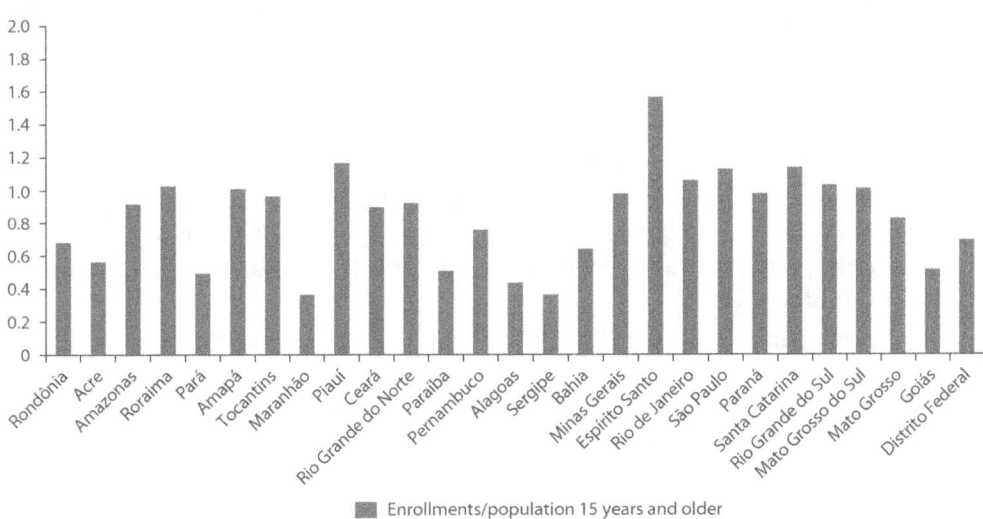

Source: Censo Escolar 2013.

years old; they are about 52 percent male; they are predominantly white; and they have completed an average of 12.25 years of schooling. Interestingly, the dropout rates among students in the technical education tracks are lower than those enrolled in academic upper secondary (24.7 percent versus 37.3 percent).[12] Almeida, Anazawa, and Menezes Filho (2014) also find that students in the technical track tend to come from higher socioeconomic backgrounds. Technical education in Brazil is also not a dead-end track and often attracts relatively strong students, many of whom often go on to tertiary education.

Finally, there is wide regional diversity in the prevalence of technical education across states and within states. Figure 1.7 illustrates the variation across Brazil in the percentage of the population 15 years or older that has ever pursued a technical education at the upper secondary level.

Notes

1. UNICEF 2012. http://www.unicef.org/infobycountry/brazil_statistics.html#117.
2. See Pesquisa Nacional por Amostra de Domicílios (PNAD, Household Sample National Survey), 2011, for schooling data—data are held by the Instituto Brasileiro de Geografia e Estatística (IBGE, Brazilian Institute for Geography and Statistics)— and Instituto Nacional de Estudos e Pesquisas (INEP, National Institute of Studies and Research), http://www.inep.gov.br/, and the Ministério da Educação (MEC, Ministry of Education), 2004–10, http://www.mec.gov.br/, for public spending data.
3. Schooling data provided by PNAD, 2002 and 2011 and OECD 2013. For spending on education as a percentage of GDP, see INEP-MEC, 2002–12.

4. Basic education includes two modalities: special education (educação especial) for people with disabilities and youth and adult education (educação de jovens e adultos, EJA). The latter targets those who stopped studying before finishing basic education.
5. For information on ISCED, see OECD (2012).
6. See PNAD/IBGE.
7. Figures provided by INEP 2013, 2014.
8. OECD Education at a Glance 2014.
9. International Standard Classification of Education (ISCED-12).
10. See Censo Escolar (School Census)/INEP, 2007, 2011 and 2013. The Censo Escolar (2007, 2008, 2011 and 2012) is produced by INEP and MEC, http://portal.inep.gov.br/basica-censo.
11. Schwartzman and Castro (2013) compare the Brazilian system with other country systems.
12. Fundação Itau Social Programa Avaliação Economica de Projectos Sociais, http://www.fundacaoitausocial.org.br.

References

Almeida, Rita, Jere Behrman, and David Robalino, eds. 2011. *The Right Skills for the Job? Rethinking Training Policies for Workers*. Washington, DC: World Bank.

Almeida, Rita, Leandro Anazawa, and Naercio Menezes Filho. 2014. "Ministério Do Trabalho e Emprego, Brasil, e pelo Banco Mundial." World Bank, Washington, DC.

Bruns, Barbara, David Evans, and Javier Luque. 2012. *Achieving World-Class Education in Brazil: The Next Agenda*. Washington, DC: World Bank.

Censo Escolar, Brazil. 2013. INEP (Instituto Nacional de Estudos e Pesquisas Educacionais/ National Institute of Studies and Research); MEC (Ministério da Educação/Ministry of Education), Brazil. http://portal.inep.gov.br/basica-censo.

INEP (Instituto Nacional de Estudos e Pesquisas Educacionais/National Institute of Studies and Research). 2013. MEC (Ministério da Educação/Ministry of Education), Brazil. http://www.inep.gov.br/.

INEP (Instituto Nacional de Estudos e Pesquisas Educacionais; National Institute of Studies and Research). 2014. MEC (Ministério da Educação; Ministry of Education), Brazil. http://www.inep.gov.br/.

INEP (Instituto Nacional de Estudos e Pesquisas Educacionais/National Institute of Studies and Research). 2015. MEC (Ministério da Educação/Ministry of Education), Brazil. http://www.inep.gov.br/.

Menezes Filho, Naercio. 2012. *Apagão de mão de obra qualificada?: As profissões eo mercado de trabalho brasileiro entre 2000 e 2010*. São Paulo: Centro de Políticas Públicas do INSPER.

OECD (Organisation for Economic Co-operation and Development). 2011. *Learning for Jobs: Pointers for Policy Development: OECD Reviews of Vocational Education and Training*. Directorate for Education, Education and Training Policy Division. http://www.oecd.org/edu/skills-beyond-school/48078260.pdf.

_____. 2012. *Education at a Glance: OECD Indicators*. http://www.uis.unesco.org/Education/Documents/oecd-eag-2012-en.pdf.

PNAD (Pesquisa Nacional por Amostra de Domicílios/National Household Sample Survey). 2011. IBGE (Instituto Brasileiro de Geografia e Estatistica/Brazilian Insitute for Geography and Statistics), Brazil.

Schwartzman, Simon, and Claudio Moura de Castro. 2013. "Estudo e Trabalho da Juventude Brasileira." Working paper, Instituto de Estudo do Trabalho e Sociedade (IETS).

UNESCO. 1997. International Standard Classification of Education-ISCED 1997: November 1997. NY: UNESCO.

CHAPTER 2

Selected Design Features and Implementation Arrangements of the VET System in Brazil

Introduction

This chapter is a more detailed review of the design and structure of the existing vocational and technical education and training (VET) system in Brazil, focusing on upper secondary education (ensino técnico, technical education). In particular, it describes in more detail the following: the different modalities and tracks in which VET programs are offered in Brazil; a typology of technical education courses; modes of delivery; the main VET providers; eligibility criteria; the VET regulatory framework, including certification of competencies and teacher selection and compensation; spending and funding of technical education; and the monitoring and evaluation of the technical education system. This chapter also provides a more detailed description of the Programa Nacional de Acesso ao Ensino Técnico e Emprego (PRONATEC, National Program for Access to Technical Education and Employment). This description is complemented with a brief description of the existing state-level programs (such as those in Minas Gerais and São Paulo) that have been implemented at the state level and that have started successful reforms at the subnational level.

VET Tracks and Program Modalities

In Brazil, both public and private providers offer programs characterized by an enormous variety of modalities and duration. Generally, however, these programs can be separated into three groups based on a student's level of educational attainment, program duration, and the sequence of academic and technical programs:

- Cursos tecnológicos (technological education) at the tertiary level, two to three years in length

Figure 2.1 Vocational and Technical Education and Training (VET) Program Enrollments as Percentage of Total Enrollments in VET: Brazil, 2007

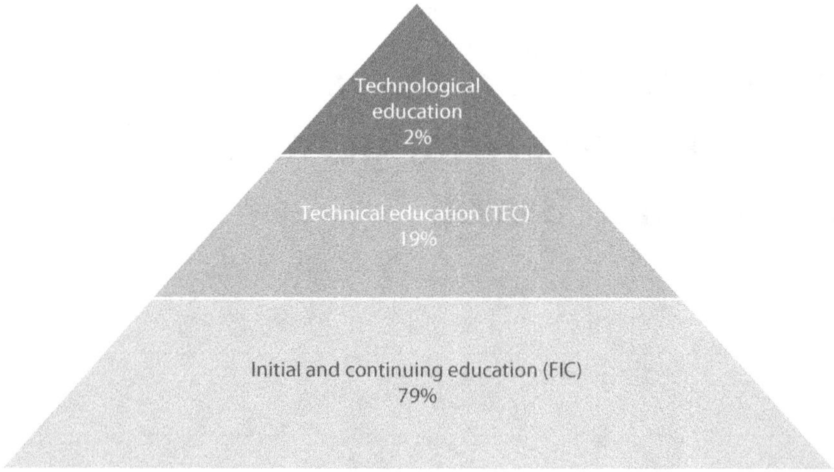

- Technological education 2%
- Technical education (TEC) 19%
- Initial and continuing education (FIC) 79%

Source: Almeida et al. 2015, based on Pesquisa Nacional por Amostra de Domicílios (PNAD, Household Sample National Survey), 2007.

- Ensino técnico (technical education) at the upper secondary level, usually completed in four years
- Cursos formação inicial e continuada (FICs, initial and continuing training courses), which are short-term programs or individual courses that do not confer an academic-level certification.

Almeida et al. (2015) use the 2007 Pesquisa Nacional por Amostra de Domicílios (PNAD, Household Sample National Survey) to show that about 79 percent of students in vocational programs nationwide are enrolled in courses classified as FICs. As noted, FICs are short-term programs, most of which are designed for individuals who have dropped out of formal schooling and are either unemployed or work in unskilled or low-skilled occupations. FICs are designed to match immediate employer needs with workers' capabilities and to quickly respond to changes in the labor market. According to figure 2.1, in 2007 the enrollment in FICs was about four times the enrollment in technical education.

Technical education (ensino técnico) consists of VET programs that complement an academic upper secondary education. These technical education programs are offered in three modalities, all of which are connected to academic secondary education and are categorized based on the sequence of academic and technical programs and the way a student registers for each:

- Técnico integrado. Vocational education combined with general education (ensino médio integrado ao profissionalizante), in which the student completes

only one upper secondary program that includes both general academic and technical courses.
- Técnico concomitante. Vocational education is given simultaneously with general academic secondary education (ensino médio concomitante ao profissionalizante), but the general academic program is taken independently of the technical one and often in a different institution—in other words, the student has two independent and separate program registrations (the reverse is not valid because the student must complete the secondary level to be able to receive a professional certification after completing a technical education program).
- Subsequente. Vocational education is pursued after completion of an academic upper secondary program in high school, although not necessarily immediately after (ensino profissionalizante subsequente ao ensino médio). The prerequisite for this modality is the completion of an academic upper secondary education.

The integrado and concomitante modalities are completed by students concurrently with an academic upper secondary program. In the concomitante modality, however, technical courses tend to be offered in the afternoon, whereas in the subsequente modality courses tend to be offered in the evenings to allow students to work during the day.

As illustrated in figure 2.1, technical programs (including the three modalities just listed) account for 19 percent of total enrollment in VET. Technical programs usually last two years when taken in the concomitante and subsequente modalities and four years in the integrado modality. The remaining 2 percent of enrollment corresponds with technological education. Technological education is considered a tertiary education level and can be pursued after completing any type of upper secondary program. It typically is two to three years in duration and often requires that a student pass an entrance examination to qualify.

As of 2007, the subsequente modality accounted for about 53 percent of technical education enrollments. In Brazil, concomitante and integrado account for approximately 21 percent and 23 percent, respectively. The prevalence of subsequente also indicates that Brazilian students in technical courses are, on average, older than expected for the upper secondary level.[1]

A Typology of Technical Courses

Within the different levels of VET—FICs, technical education, and technological education— enrollments in different programs can vary greatly. A disaggregation of the share of workforce by level of VET achieved reveals that although the majority of VET-trained workers end up in the automotive industry, these are also mostly students from FIC courses—the short-term training and professional qualification courses. At the level of technical education, however, the industry with the largest share of workers with technical graduates is commerce and services, followed by gas and petroleum, and at the technological level the highest percentage is found in finance (see figure 2.2).

By contrast, figure 2.3, shows the largest enrollments in 2010 through Bolsa Formação Estudante (Student Training Scholarship), the federal PRONATEC scholarship program for low-income technical education students. Figure 2.3 describes the courses with the highest enrollments through Bolsa Formação.

Figure 2.2 Industries with Highest Percentage of Vocational and Technical Education and Training (VET) Graduates by Level of VET: Brazil, 2007

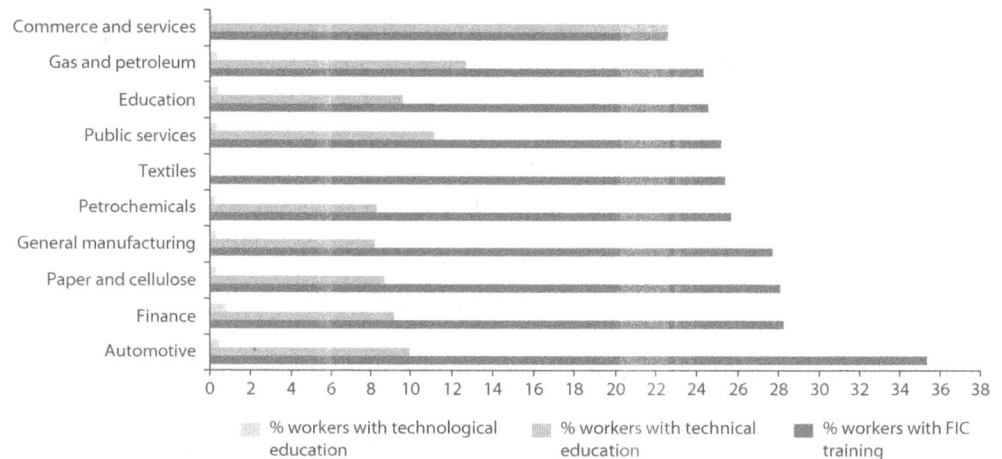

Sources: Based on Neri 2010 and Pesquisa Nacional por Amostra de Domicílios (PNAD, Household Sample National Survey), 2007.
Note: VET = vocational and technical education and training; FIC = curso de formação inicial e continuada (initial and continued training course).

Figure 2.3 Technical Courses with Largest Enrollments through Bolsa Formação: Brazil, 2010

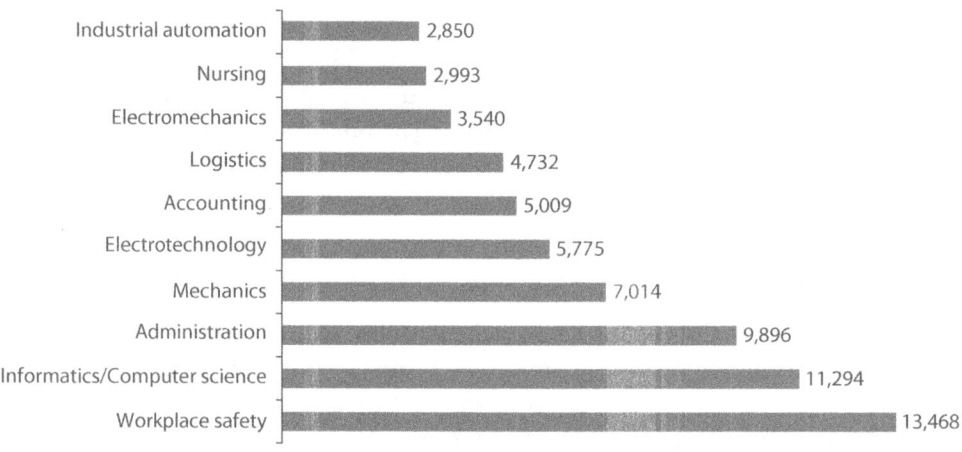

Source: Data provided by Sistema Nacional de Informações da Educação Profissional e Tecnológica (SISTEC, National System of Professional and Technological Education), 2010, and published by Ministério da Educação (MEC, Ministry of Education)–Secretaria de Educação Profissional e Tecnológica (SETEC, Office of Vocational and Technological Education).

Modes of Delivery: Classroom, Distance, and Workplace Learning

Most technical programs in Brazil are classroom-based, but enrollments in distance learning are rising for all forms of vocational education, including technical education, and through all types of providers (private and public schools, including federal and state programs). Indeed, distance learning is emerging as one of the best options for offering vocational education in many regions of Brazil that have low population density and where long distances from school can make it difficult for students to attend daily classes, such as in the north of Brazil. Distance learning can facilitate vocational education for both provider and student. Students can access learning from home, and providers need fewer locations in low-density or hard-to-access areas to reach these populations.[2]

Because of the rapid expansion planned under PRONATEC, the program includes an important distance "e-learning" component that draws on the existing experiences of this type across the country. Under PRONATEC, E-TEC Brasil will expand the VET network to more remote regions in the country. E-TEC's e-learning centers, located in Federal Institutes and universities, Serviço Nacional de Aprendizagem Industrial (SENAI, National Service of Industrial Learning), Serviço Nacional de Aprendizagem Comercial (SENAC, National Commercial Training Service), Serviço Nacional de Aprendizagem Rural (SENAR, National Rural Education Service), and Serviço Nacional de Aprendizagem do Transporte (SENAT, National Transportation Learning Service), are shown in map 2.1.

Workplace learning in the form of apprenticeships, or estágios, is a third mode of delivery that complements classroom delivery at the level of secondary technical education. Apprenticeships, however, are neither uniformly offered throughout VET in Brazil nor required for a student to complete his or her technical education and receive certification. According to the Catalogo Nacional de Cursos Técnicos (National Catalogue of Technical Education), apprenticeships and workplace learning can be carried out in addition to the required number of hours of classroom instruction, but not in place of classroom time. Data on the frequency and availability of apprenticeships are not readily available on a national level, however, and the decision to require an apprenticeship for completion of technical education is left to the discretion of the VET provider. The decision to require an apprenticeship is often determined by the availability of such opportunities in the area in which VET is being offered. The Lei de Aprendizagem of 2000 legally mandates that the total number of professional employees of all medium and large companies must include students (5–15 percent of the total) for a period of up to two years and that they should be paid at least the minimum wage. However, these opportunities are not exclusive to technical education students or available in all regions and municipalities.[3] Sistema S has generally included an apprenticeship as a mandatory part of its technical education programs, but recently some institutions in Sistema S removed the requirement for some of their technical education programs because of lack of enough apprenticeship opportunities for all students.

Map 2.1 Location of E-TEC Brazil Centers

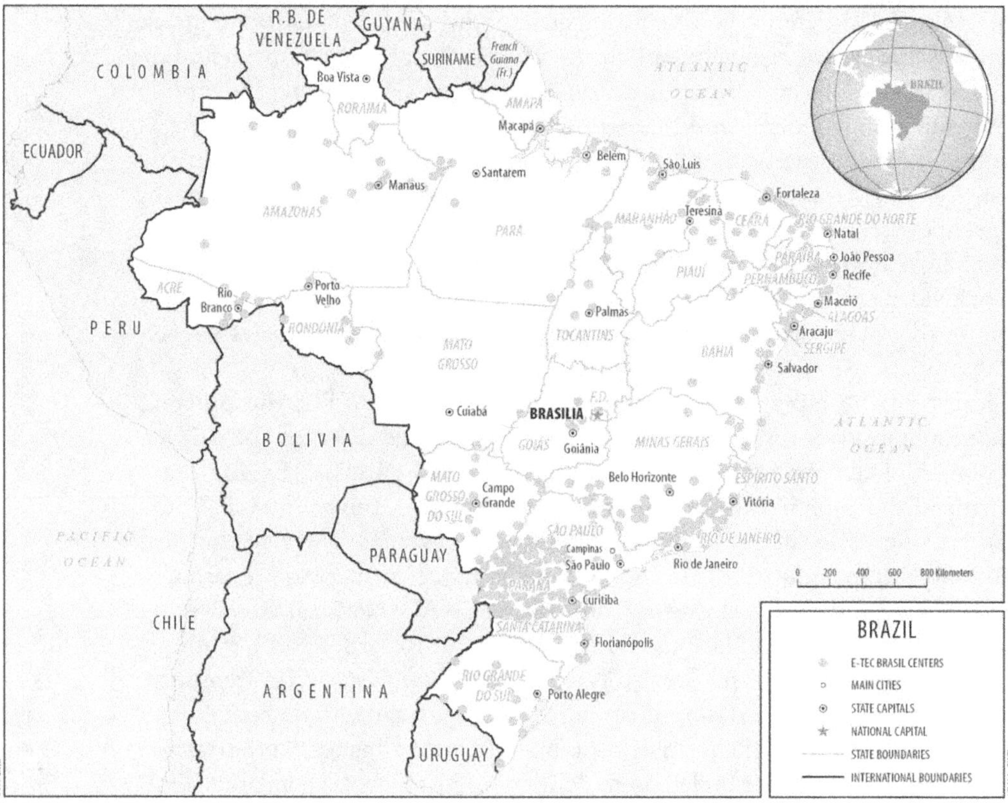

Source: PRONATEC/MEC website.

Main VET Providers

The main providers of VET programs in Brazil are public providers (including the federal institutes and state governments) and Sistema S (for example, SENAI and SENAC). Municipalities also offer vocational education, but such programs represent a very small percentage of VET enrollments. Figure 2.4, illustrates that these three public providers together account for approximately 40 percent of enrollment in VET. The remaining 60 percent of enrollment in VET at all levels is covered by private schools. Private enrollment is distributed among the more than 2,000 private establishments. As result, the concentration of students in any one private provider is much lower than in the top three main public providers.[4] Each one of the three main providers—federal, state, and Sistema S—offers programs at the three different duration and qualification levels: FICs, technical education, and technological courses.

The private sector also provides a substantial part of technical education. Figure 2.5, further breaks downs the distribution of enrollments across providers as of 2014. Figure 2.5, in contrast to figure 2.4, considers Sistema S a pri-

Figure 2.4 Total Enrollment in Vocational and Technical Education and Training (VET) by Type of VET Provider: Brazil, 2007

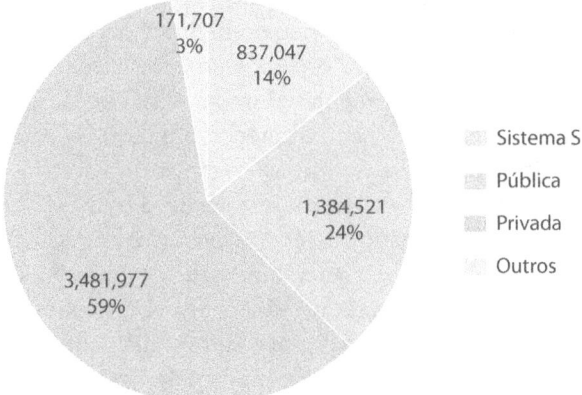

- Sistema S
- Pública
- Privada
- Outros

171,707 — 3%
837,047 — 14%
1,384,521 — 24%
3,481,977 — 59%

Source: Based on Pesquisa Nacional por Amostra de Domicílios (PNAD, Household Sample National Survey), 2007.

Figure 2.5 Enrollment in Technical Education by Provider Type: Brazil, 2014

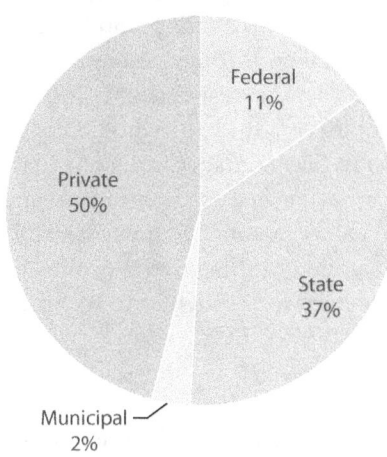

- Federal 11%
- State 37%
- Municipal 2%
- Private 50%

Sources: Based on Censo Escolar (School Census); Instituto Nacional de Estudos e Pesquisas (INEP, National Institute of Studies and Research), 2014.

vate provider (the public-private nature of Sistema S results in differences in reporting and aggregation), and data are also from different years.[5] According to figure 2.5, private enrollments account for 50 percent of total enrollments (which includes programs and courses provided by Sistema S), state VET systems for 37 percent, and federal VET systems for 11 percent. Municipal level providers account for only 2 percent of total enrollments. All VET providers have to be accredited by the Ministério da Educação (MEC, Ministry of Education) or by a state level accreditation agent (see the next section for more details).

Within FIC courses, the Ministério do Trabalho e do Emprego (MTE, Ministry of Labor and Employment) and the state secretariats of labor have their own short-duration training programs. These are considered qualification programs, which consist of short-term training for a predefined occupation. They are designed to meet a very specific industry or local demand. These types of short-duration courses are not organized or regulated under MEC because it is unlikely that the courses will be standardized and offered as a nationally catalogued VET program. As a result, these short-duration programs under ministries or secretariats often do not have skills certifications approved by MEC or another educational agent. Contracted educational institutions usually provide these short-duration programs, most often in partnership with the ministry or state secretariat sponsoring the program and main providers of FIC programs.[6]

Student payment for VET also varies by provider, state, and municipality, and the profile of the student (that is, whether the student is a beneficiary of a federal or state social program that offers VET free of charge). Any public institution that is part of the federal or state networks offers VET programs to students at no cost. In Sistema S, however, the cost can vary; some students will study at no cost thanks to subsidies provided by public social programs such as Bolsa Formação Trabalhador (Worker Training Scholarship), or they will qualify for the new Free of Charge VET Vacancies Agreement signed by Sistema S and MEC. If an employer pays for VET courses, typically FICs, taken through Sistema S, the students will not be directly charged; payment is the responsibility of the employer soliciting the courses for his or her employees. Students who do not fit into one of these beneficiary categories and wish to take courses through Sistema S will be charged, although the amount will vary according to the program and state. Additional student financing for technical education is now available through an expansion of the Fundo de Financiamento ao Estudante do Ensino Superior (FIES, Fund for Financing Higher Education for Students) to technical education students under PRONATEC (known as FIES-TEC).

Federal System of Vocational Education

Since 2003, the federal education system has undergone a large expansion. From the beginning of the last century until 2002, 140 federal vocational institutes were built, and between 2003 and 2010, 214 new institutes were established. In 2008 the rate of expansion increased, shortly after the launch of the new Fundo de Manutenção e Desenvolvimento da Educação Básica e de Valorização dos Profissionais da Educação (FUNDEB, Fund for the Maintenance and Development of Basic Education and Enhancement of Education Professionals). The new program resulted in a very substantial increase in federal funds committed to all stages of basic education, including funds for educação jovens e adultos (EJA, youth and adult education). Currently, 527 federal units provide VET (at least one unit per state), and they account for more than 400 federally provided vacancies across Brazil (*Source:* MEC Website).

Nevertheless, the federal education network continues to be concentrated in a few regions, leaving the midwest and north with very few units. Even though this concentration is consistent with the concentration of population across the country, in the north, with its sparse population and poor transportation, many people encounter severe difficulties in accessing Federal institutes. There, distance education will likely play an important role in providing greater access to VET via home access (although issues of connectivity and prestige of distance education will have to be considered). Map 2.2 illustrates the concentration of the federal system of vocational education, which includes the Federal Institutes of Vocational Education, technological universities, federal centers of technological education (CEFETs), and technical schools that are financially or administratively dependent on federal universities. Each dot or square in map 2.2 represents one of these institutions.

Sistema S

The National Service for Apprenticeship, more commonly referred to as Sistema S, was created in the 1940s in response to the mobilization of business entities, industry associations, and representatives of economic sectors seeking to train the professionals they needed because those in the market were of

Map 2.2 Federal System of Vocational Education: Brazil, 2010

Source: Ministério da Educação (MEC, Ministry of Education), 2010.

insufficient quality and quantity. Among the major institutions that make up Sistema S, several were created in the mid-1940s. These include Servico Social da Industria (SESI, Industry Social Service the National Service of Industrial Training (SENAI, Serviço Nacional de Aprendizagem Industrial), the National Service for Commercial Training (SENAC, Serviço Nacional de Aprendizagem Comercial) and Serviço Social do Comércio (SESC, Social Service of Commerce). In the 1980s, the Serviço Brasileiro de Apoio às Micro e Pequenas Empresas (SEBRAE, Brazilian Support Service for Micro and Small Enterprises) was created to respond to the needs of small and medium enterprises, and the Instituto Nacional de Colonização e Reforma Agrária (INCRA, National Institute of Colonization and Agrarian Reform) was created to administer land reform issues. The remaining institutions that make up Sistema S were created in the 1990s and include Serviço Social do Transporte (SEST, Transportation Social Service) and Serviço Nacional de Aprendizagem do Transporte (SENAT, the National Service for Transportation Training); Serviço Nacional de Aprendizagem do Cooperativismo (SESCOOP, National Service for Cooperative Learning); and the Serviço Nacional de Aprendizagem Rural (SENAR, National Service for Rural Training). Today, the objectives of Sistema S are to enhance the quality of the lives of workers through the provision of vocational and technical education, as well as health care and leisure. Each institution in Sistema S is financed mainly through payroll taxes collected from the industries or economic sector linked to each institution. As noted earlier, however, whether students pay for vocational and technical education provided through Sistema S is dependent on a number of factors. Some students will study free of charge through subsidies provided by public social programs such as Bolsa Formação Trabalhador or as a qualifying student for the new Free of Charge VET Vacancies Agreement signed between Sistema S and MEC. If an employer pays for VET courses taken through Sistema S, the students also will not be charged. Students who do not fall into one of these beneficiary categories and wish to take courses through Sistema S will pay to enroll in a program, but the cost will vary according to the program or state. Although Sistema S is linked to specific industry associations, the VET programs offered are generally open to all students, with the exception of certain training programs sponsored by specific employers or VET programs with high demand and so subject to selection or eligibility criteria.

Among these institutions, SENAI and SENAC stand out for being the most important providers of FIC, technological, and technical education. In 2010 total enrollments in these two services accounted for approximately 1.7 million students (excluding tertiary-level enrollments), according to information provided by these institutions.[7]

Serviço Nacional de Aprendizagem Industrial (SENAI)
SENAI, a member of the Confederação Nacional da Indústria (CNI, National Confederation of Industry), supports 29 different technological areas through training of human resources and the provision of services such as support to the

productive sector, laboratory services, applied research, and information technology. SENAI dedicates 797 operating units to VET. Of these, 471 are fixed units that offer courses maintained by their 27 regional departments. The remaining 326 are mobile units of professional education services that respond to productive sectors located in more distant and hard-to-access regions of the country.

Currently, SENAI offers 1,623 training courses and 1,069 technical courses, organized into 26 occupational areas. It also provides an additional 76 higher education courses and 119 postgraduate courses. SENAI has its own system of distance education (220 courses).

In 2010 enrollment in professional education offered by SENAI totaled 2.36 million students, 346,100 of whom received this education free of charge. Total student enrollment by type of program is as follows: initial and continuing professional education, 561,364; basic training for industry, 135,760; basic professional qualification, 377,298; technical courses, 147,997; tertiary education, 11,713; tertiary education (post–upper secondary), 6,572; and further training, 1.12 million.

Serviço Nacional de Aprendizagem Comercial (SENAC)

SENAC, a member of the Confederação Nacional do Comércio de Bens, Serviços e Turismo (CNC, National Confederation of Trade in Goods, Services, and Tourism) has become a reference in professional education and knowledge production for the goods trading market, services sector, and tourism in Brazil. It consists of 573 operating units. Of these, 527 offer technological education in nine axes: environment, health and safety, educational support, business and management, hospitality and leisure, information and communication, infrastructure, cultural management and design, and natural resources.

SENAC offers VET courses in the following modes of delivery: classroom learning, distance learning, and partial online courses. These courses range from initial and continuing training programs (FIC) to technical education (upper secondary) or technological education (tertiary). In 2010 the total enrollment in SENAC courses was 1.15 million; the total number of completed enrollments was 923,951; and the total number of vacancies was 1.12 million.

State-Level Schools

As outlined in the Lei de Diretrizes de Base, states have the primary responsibility for the provision of secondary education, including technical education. As a result, in Brazil 85 percent of secondary education overall takes place in state-level schools. However, there is diversity across states in the importance of state-level schools in technical education. In some states, technical education is mainly administered by the state secretary of education. In others such as São Paulo and Ceará, technical education is administered by the state secretary of science and technology.

Box 2.1 describes the case of São Paulo, where the provision of VET is expanding at the state level under the aegis of the secretary of economic

Box 2.1   The Experience of São Paulo: Paula Souza Center

Centro Estadual de Educação Técnica e Tecnológica Paula Souza (Paula Souza State Center for Technical and Technological Education) is the largest state institution dedicated to technical and vocational education at the secondary and tertiary levels in Brazil. It is composed of 211 technical schools with 216,000 students and 56 tertiary-level technical institutions, with 65,000 students distributed across 161 municipalities in São Paulo State. Although it offers good-quality programs in all 22 technical areas offered in Brazil, 62 percent of its students concentrate on construction, production, and mathematics and computation. Students are selected through a competitive process, but affirmative action policies also ensure that students from low-income backgrounds and underrepresented groups have access to the programs offered by the network. As of 2012, Centro Paula Souza covered about 42 percent of all technical education in the state.

Centro Paula Souza works closely with the private sector—an arrangement that produces benefits for both its students as well as for employers and the São Paulo economy as a whole. Studies have shown that a significant number of students from Centro Paula Souza go on to study in universities, and those who choose to go directly into the labor market easily find jobs. By 2012, 62 percent of the 2010 graduates were working in their field of study, and only 7.8 percent were unemployed.

The quality of the center's programs and classes seems to correlate with its students' results on national exams. In the Exame Nacional do Ensino Medio (ENEM, National Exam for Upper Secondary Education), which evaluates the general competencies of all upper secondary students, including technical students, 12 of the 50 top-performing institutions were members of the Centro Paula Souza network.

Source: Schwartzman and Castro (2013).

---

development, science, and technology through the development of the Centro Estadual de Educação Técnica e Tecnológica Paula Souza (Paula Souza Center).

Eligibility Criteria: Merit, Ordering and Priority Criteria

As described, many courses provided by the public network of federal and state schools or by Sistema S are free of charge. Among this group, there is often excess demand for VET programs or individual courses, especially at the technical education level. In these cases, institutions apply eligibility and selection criteria, which differ between public and private networks. This section briefly describes those differences.

Public VET institutions in federal and state networks usually favor merit criteria for possible applicants—that is, those interested in applying to a public VET Institution take an entrance exam provided by the institution and must earn a minimum grade to be eligible for consideration. The highest-scoring-candidates are selected. In Sistema S, merit criteria or allocation of enrollment on a first come, first served basis (that is, using an ordering criterion in which all those seeking enrollment register for a program or course, and preference is given by order of registration) may be employed.[8]

Both the federal network and Sistema S also use quotas for students from public schools to ensure ethnic and socioeconomic diversity. After organizing the candidates in order of preference (by merit or on a first come, first served basis), these schools enforce a quota of allocating 50 percent of places to students from public schools and, in addition, requiring that these are allocated across Afro-descendants and indigenous peoples in the same proportion as in the state population.[9]

Many of the state and municipal networks of education, however, have their own priority criteria or quotas. At Centro Paula Souza, São Paulo schools account for almost one-third of national public enrollments in technical courses. Students from public schools receive a bonus of 10 percent on their entrance exam test scores, and candidates who self-declare as Afro-descendants receive a bonus of 3 percent on their test scores. These bonuses can be cumulative, totaling, for example, 13 percent for Afro-descendants coming from public school (see table 2.1 for details on eligibility criteria).

Table 2.1 Eligibility Criteria for Vocational Education (Secondary Level), State of São Paulo

		\multicolumn{3}{c}{Elegibility Criteria for Vocational Education - Secondary Level}		
		Merit Criteria	**Ordering/ Randomization Criteria**	**Priority Criteria/ Quotas**
Public Systems	**Federal Institutes**	Entrance Exam (Vestibulinho)	NO	Quotas: 50% reserved to students from public school, distributed as population composition african descent and indigenous people)
	State Agents	Entrance Exam (Vestibulinho)	NO	SP-Centro Paula Souza: bonus for students from public schools (10%) and african descent (3%)
Sistema S	**SENAI/SP**	Entrance Exam		Age (for special cases), Low income, PRONATEC
	SENAC/SP	NO	Ordering	Age (for special cases), Low income, PRONATEC
New Programs	**Pronatec**	NO	YES	Beneficiaries of partners's programs: MDS, MTE, MinTur
	Vence / SP	Vence Integrado: when partner is Centro Paula Souza	VENCE Integrado when partner is IFSP, and Concomitante - Ramdomization	Vence Integrado - student living close to school

Sources: Based on information from the Secretaria de Estado da Educação de São Paulo (SEE, São Paulo State Secretary of Education), Centro Paula Souza, Serviço Nacional de Aprendizagem Industrial/São Paulo (SENAI/SP, National Service of Industrial Learning), Serviço Nacional de Aprendizagem Comercial/São Paulo (SENAC/SP, National Commercial Training Service), and Instituto Federal de São Paulo (IFSP, Federal Institute of São Paulo).
Note: PRONATEC = Programa Nacional de Acesso ao Ensino Técnico e Emprego (National Program for Access to Technical Education and Employment); MDS = Ministério do Desenvolvimento Social e Combate à Fome (Ministry of Social Development and Fight against Hunger); MTE = Ministério do Trabalho e Emprego (Ministry of Labor and Employment); MinTur = Ministério de Turismo (Ministry of Tourism).

Within Sistema S, places are also reserved for low-income students. According to the 2009 Free of Charge VET Vacancies Agreement between MEC and Sistema S, places reserved for low-income students would grow until 2014 or until the resources allocated to these places reached one-third of the total funds drawn compulsorily from the payrolls of the industries participating in Sistema S.

The selection procedures used for the federal PRONATEC program and the state-level São Paulo Vence program illustrate additional ways of selecting and prioritizing students. PRONATEC, under Bolsa Formação and Bolsa Formação Trabalhador, includes VET courses offered by the Federal Institutes or Sistema S that are designed and reserved for private companies or a partner ministry such as the Ministério do Desenvolvimento Social e Combate à Fome (MDS, Ministry of Social Development and Fight against Hunger), MTE, and the Ministério de Turismo (MinTur, Ministry of Tourism). Places may be reserved for these particular PRONATEC students in the courses offered. Extra places not filled by PRONATEC students may be offered to others who are interested.

The Vence program provided by the secretary of education of São Paulo, for example, focuses on technical education and is divided into Vence Integrado and Vence Concomitante. Vence Integrado uses two variations on student selection. Under the Instituto Federal de São Paulo partnership, students are selected randomly when there is excess demand for a program, whereas the partnership with Centro Paula Souza applies merit criteria via an entrance exam. To participate in Vence Concomitante, youth enrolled in secondary education apply for a VET program and an institution that offers that program. Where there is excess demand, students are selected randomly.

VET Regulatory Framework: Bridging Occupations and Courses

VET regulation has a legal basis in the Lei de Diretrizes e Bases da Educação Nacional (LDB, Law of National Guidelines for Educationrr) of 1996 and Decreto No. 5.154 of 2004, which regulates LDB regarding the VET.[10] These laws and decrees stipulate that the federal Conselho Nacional de Educação (CNE, National Board of Education) is the main regulatory agent responsible for VET. However, each Brazilian state also has its own regulatory framework, which operates in accordance with, and subject to, CNE decisions. These state-level Conselhos Estaduais de Educação (CEEs, Boards of Education) are the agents responsible for VET regulation in each state. At the federal level, MEC is still responsible for designing education policy, including VET and its monitoring and evaluation. The state secretariats of education or science and technology have similar functions to MEC, but only at the state level.

MEC is also responsible for organizing and disseminating the national catalogue of technical courses (Catálogo Nacional de Cursos Técnico). The catalogue lists the set of nationally authorized programs and courses and the minimum academic requirements that must be offered by providers for each. Nevertheless, there is still considerable variation in the quality of providers and courses and

VET programs nationwide. The catalogue defines the main activities that graduates of one of these programs should be able to undertake; the market or field that offers opportunities for that profession; the infrastructure required to teach courses in the particular field; and the recommended program duration. However, the detailed contents of the programs, including whether they require an on-the-job learning component, are at the discretion of the providers.[11]

It is important to highlight, however, that the catalogue is not well linked to the Classificação Basica de Ocupações (CBO, Basic Classification of Occupations) created in 2002 and administered by the Ministério do Trabalho e Emprego (MTE, Ministry of Labor and Employment). The CBO identifies, describes, and classifies occupations available in the Brazilian labor market according to the International Statistical Classification of Occupations (ISCO-88). Looking ahead, it is critical to identify within the existing occupations the competencies they require and to subsequently match these with the appropriate VET courses designed to develop these same competencies. This implies a much greater articulation between the CBO and the catalogue. The Ministry of Labor and Employment and MEC have already begun discussing the link between the two, but the process is incipient and hampered by criticism of the CBO's listing of occupations. Critics say it is quite restricted, and the process of creation and elimination of occupations impedes the dynamism of the private sector.

Certification of Competencies in Technical Education

In Brazil, there is no formal certification framework, but the Federal Institutes and the network of VET providers play an important role. Article 42 of the 1996 Lei de Diretrizes e Bases da Educação states, "The knowledge gained in professional education, including at work, may be subject to assessment, recognition and certification for continuity or completion of studies." This legal mandate was established in 1996, but it was only in 2004 that the National Board of Education (CNE, Conselho Nacional de Educação) gave the Federal Institutes of VET responsibility for assessing and recognizing competencies previously acquired in training or in the practical exercise of an occupation.

In 2007, the CERTIFIC Network (Rede: Certificação Profissional e Formação Inicial e Continuada, Network: Initial Training and Professional Certification and Continuation) was created by a ministerial decree originating from MEC and the Ministry of Labor and Employment. The goals were to execute the CNE mandate and improve the existing certification system. The CERTIFIC Network is composed of the following institutions:

- *Institutos Federais de Educação, Ciência e Tecnologia (Federal Institutes of Education, Science, and Technology)*. They develop and implement certification programs and are responsible for carrying out the accreditation of institutions for the same activities.

- *Public institutions of VET, Sistema S, and VET schools linked to trade unions or nongovernmental organizations.* They deploy and develop certification programs and training for the CERTIFIC Network.
- *Government agencies and nongovernmental organizations.* They have responsibilities related to education, certification, metrology, standardization, and inspection of professional practice, and support the operation of the CERTIFIC Network.

CERTIFIC also certifies knowledge that has been acquired by employees on the job in a wide variety of fields such as fisheries and aquaculture, music, construction, tourism and hospitality, and electronics. Although participants in the program must be over 18 years old, they do not need proof of previous professional experience, and there is no restriction on the level of schooling required to participate. Participation in this program is free, and there are an unlimited number of places. Applicants simply have to apply for a knowledge assessment. Those who are approved via a knowledge assessment receive a diploma, certifying the knowledge and skills they have acquired in that particular field or industry. Those who are not approved may attend a CERTIFIC qualification course to improve their skills and eventually obtain certification. This qualification course can last up to 160 hours for those who have already completed basic education and two to three years for those who have not yet completed basic education. In the latter, the program includes basic education in addition to vocational subjects.

VET Teacher Selection, Career Trajectories, and Compensation

According to the 2012 Censo Escolar (School Census), there are almost 72,000 teacher positions (funções docentes) in technical education (upper secondary level) in Brazil. More than half of these positions (58 percent) are in the subsequente modality, 33 percent in integrado, and 8 percent in concomitante. In general, VET teachers are university-educated (91 percent of these teachers have graduated from a tertiary education program). Fifty-three percent teach in private institutions, 30 percent in state networks, and 13 percent in the federal network.

Although technical education is part of Brazil's basic education system, technical education in the public education system differs greatly from that in the traditional academic schools. First, the qualifications of teachers in the two main providers of technical education—public schools and Sistema S—are typically higher than those in academic upper secondary schools as well as the qualifications of VET teachers in the private sector. Teacher selection is also carried out differently in the public and the private systems, including in Sistema S. The following sections explain briefly the main similarities and differences.

Public School Systems

In the public system of technical education (federal and state levels), teacher salaries and career trajectories tend to be higher and better than in the general academic secondary school system. In general, the wages tend to be higher, and there is also more job stability even when compared with private VET providers. For example, in São Paulo public VET teachers from VET Federal Institutes have a career development plan, providing a level of stability and prestige that attracts relatively well-qualified candidates to the profession.

In the Federal Institutes, and in almost all state schools that provide technical education, the number of teaching posts is determined by the needs of particular courses and the corresponding field of study. In general, posts can be categorized into three types of time commitments: 20 hours per week, 40 hours per week, or an exclusive commitment.

Teachers are usually selected by public tender, which takes into account level of academic training, results from specific knowledge assessments, and previous teaching performance.[12] The professional selected by the tender must also complete a probationary period. Upon successful completion of this period, the teacher receives a stable employment contract, meaning that his or her employment cannot be terminated except in light of significant evidence supporting termination.

The professional development and wage increases of VET teachers are based on their academic degrees and professional experience. Teachers are elected by their colleagues to fill management positions, which are temporary positions lasting from two to four years. There is a monetary incentive to take up managerial positions because the bonus for a management position can be incorporated into the teacher's regular salary even after that teacher leaves the management position.

Private Providers and Sistema S

In private VET networks and in Sistema S, contracting teachers is similar to hiring professionals at any private company. Typically, private VET providers have more flexibility than public providers to hire and fire teachers. Teachers usually have a contract that establishes a monthly salary based on the number of hours worked. Private schools also differ from public institutions in organizational structure. Managers are hired specifically for management positions, and this appointment does not have a predefined length. This contrasts with the temporary status of teachers elected to management positions in the public network. Perhaps with the exception of Sistema S, the quality of teachers in private providers of VET varies greatly. In general, these teachers have lower qualifications because the lack of job stability, and the often lower wages in the private sector attract less-qualified candidates than the public providers, who can offer a more attractive package.

Spending on and Funding of Technical Education

This section briefly describes the recent total spending on and funding for technical and technological education conducted by the public system (including federal- and state-level schools) and Sistema S.

Basic Education Funding, FUNDEB

Publicly provided technical education is financed by the same funding system used for basic education: FUNDEB. FUNDEB, which has been in effect since 2007, mandates that 20 percent of total municipal and state revenues[13] be allocated to education and be held in a fund in each state.[14]

By law, the federal government contributes an additional 10 percent of this total value. Because there is a mandated minimum expenditure per student, the federal government also contributes additional resources when state and municipal revenues are not sufficient to meet the minimum contribution to FUNDEB for that particular state. This additional federal contribution is meant to reduce national inequalities.[15]

Figure 2.6, describes the main contributors to FUNDEB and how resources are allocated among state and municipal education systems.

In practice, financial resources from FUNDEB are distributed across municipal and state networks depending on each state's levels of enrollment in the basic

Figure 2.6 Brazil's Education Funding System since 2007, FUNDEB

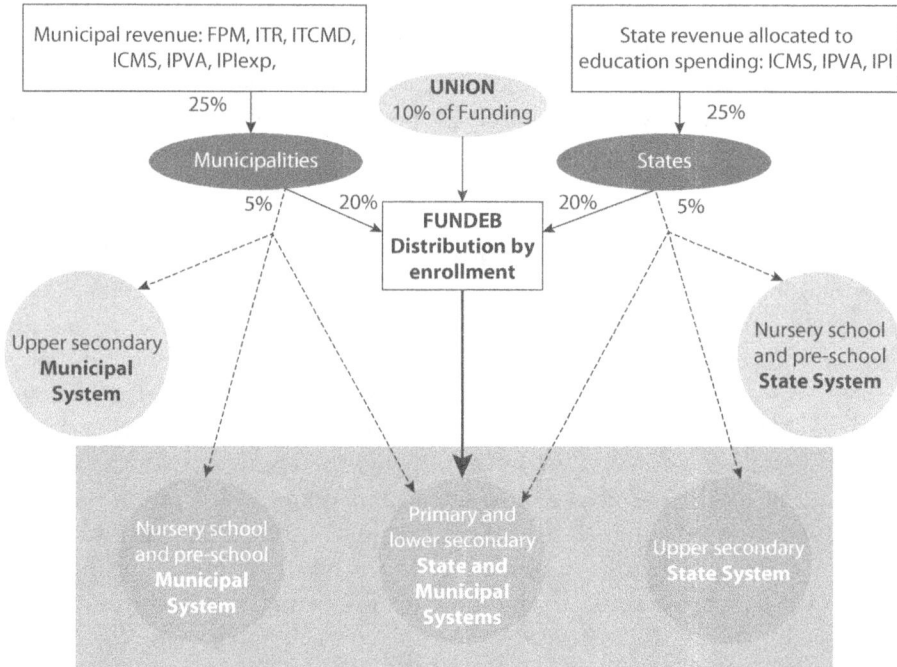

Source: Created by author, Fabiana de Felicio with information from FNDE (Fundo Nacional de Desenvolvimento da Educação)
Note: FPM= Fundo de Participação dos Municípios (Municipal Participation Fund); ITR = Imposto Territorial Rural (Rural Land Tax); ITCMD = Imposto sobre Transmissão Causa Mortis e Doações (Estate and Donations Tax); ICMS = Imposto sobre Circulação de Mercadorias e Serviços (Tax on Services and Merchandise); IPVA = Imposto sobre Propriedade de Veículos Automotores (Motor Vehicle Property Tax); IPIexp = Imposto sobre Produtos Industrializados, proporcional às exportações (Tax on Industrial Products proportional to exports); IPI = Imposto sobre Produtos Industrializados (Excise Tax); FUNDEB = Fundo de Manutenção e Desenvolvimento da Educação Básica e de Valorização dos Profissionais da Educação (Fund for the Maintenance and Development of Basic Education and Enhancement of Education Professionals).

education system. This allocation considers different weights for each education level or modality (from nursery school to upper secondary education) as a function of the primary level value (with a weigh factor equal to 1). For example, in 2012 the minimum value transferred by FUNDEB per student for upper secondary education in the integrado modality was R$2,726. This corresponds with the national minimum value in 2012 of R$2,097 multiplied by the factor 1.30 (the weight assigned to this modality relative to primary education).

This weighting system, however, does not reflect the actual per student expenditures, including for technical education. For example, the 30 percent additional resources allocated to upper secondary education for integrado does not correspond with the real difference in costs and spending between the academic secondary-level education and technical education. Table 2.2 reports the average spending per student in technical education and in regular upper secondary education, together with enrollments. According to the Sistema de Informações sobre Orçamentos Públicos em Educação (SIOPE, Information System on Public Budgets in Education), in 2008 the mean expenditure per student in technical education combined with regular upper secondary education (integrado) was three times the amount spent per student at the traditional academic secondary level.[16]

According to data from 2008, technical education was 3.1 times more expensive than general academic education at the upper secondary level. This greater cost suggests the need for a closer look at the labor market benefits of this type of technical education in both the short and the medium run. It is therefore critical that incentives to increase technical education enrollment are mapped with an effort to generate better evidence on the returns to this type of education.[17]

Federal VET System
In 2012 the budget allocated to the federal VET program was approximately R$5.04 billion. Excluding the Free of Charge VET Vacancies Agreement between MEC and Sistema S that uses Sistema S resources, this annual amount funded 1.9 million enrollments in VET in the same year, which translates to an average investment of R$4,639 per student in the federal network.

Sistema S Funding System
Sistema S is financed through a payroll tax of 2.5 percent. In 2010 this tax amounted to more than R$12 billion. These funds are given directly to the institutions that make up Sistema S: primarily SENAI (Serviço Nacional de Aprendizagem Industrial—National Service of Industrial Training), SEBRAE (Serviço Brasileiro de Apoio às Micro e Pequenas Empresas—Brazilian Support Service for Micro and Small Enterprises), SENAC (Serviço Nacional de Aprendizagem Comercial—National Service for Commercial Training), SESI (Serviço Social da Industria—Industry Social Service), SENAR (Serviço Nacional de Aprendizagem Rural—National Service for Rural Training), SENAT (Servico

Table 2.2 Public Expenditure on Upper Secondary and Technical Education and Enrollment by State: Brazil, 2008

State / Figure A1.	Public annual expenditure on education per student (R$)		Enrollment	
	Upper secondary education	Technical education[a]	Upper secondary education	Technical education[a]
Acre	101.26	5,206.27	30,844	1,572
Alagoas	1,053.99	1,147.66	96,792	6,746
Amapá	3,653.29	34,179.77	32,397	1,437
Amazonas	1,780.00	26,239.94	148,834	8,247
Bahia	1,886.87	3,072.53	568,295	12,658
Ceará	466.76	6,325.62	352,832	6,949
Distrito Federal	5,132.68	3,533.41	64,876	4,024
Espírito Santo	1,795.93	2,003.86	116,222	6,076
Goiás	3,137.07	487.45	226,856	1,294
M. G. do Sul	1,982.01	2,383.00	77,946	2,041
Maranhão	487.40	72,992.49	283,051	2,537
Mato Grosso	28.79	7,300.96	132,220	1,414
Minas Gerais	1,211.77	13,586.16	708,852	5,233
Pará	1,623.59	2,253.72	309,876	3,715
Paraíba	694.93	153.94	126,826	4,084
Paraná	2,492.73	269.20	397,654	43,151
Pernambuco	955.14	8,277.69	372,171	3,495
Piauí	1,523.62	70.08	154,691	12,617
Rio Grande do Norte	1,570.12	2,135.47	130,841	1,129
Rio Grande do Sul	1,475.34	1,456.11	369,317	32,340
Rio de Janeiro	1,185.80	7,112.92	523,912	30,582
Rondônia	1,871.14	44,654.51	54,992	139
Roraima	3,431.28	14,717.25	14,586	461
Santa Catarina	1,323.96	354.06	200,551	11,906
São Paulo	1,834.45	5,202.31	1,482,518	110,701
Sergipe	3,643.22	6,480.35	72,520	419
Tocantins	1,872.05	45.08	66,044	3,437
Brazil	**R$1,574.53**	**R44,950.38**	**7,116,516**	**318,404**

Sources: Sistema de Informações sobre Orçamentos Públicos em Educação (SIOPE, Information System on Public Budgets in Education), 2008; Censo Escolar (School Census), 2008.
a. Includes integrado, concomitante, and subsequente.

Nacional de Aprendizagem do Transporte—National Service for Transportation Training), SESCOOP (Serviço Nacional de Aprendizagem do Cooperativismo—National Service for Cooperative Learning), SEST (Serviço Social do Transporte—Transportation Social Service), and IEL (Instituto Euvaldo Lodi—Institute of Euvaldo Lodi). By law, however, three-fifths of these funds must be allocated to social services and two-fifths to learning services. In 2010 these funds accounted for almost three-quarters of total public spending on secondary education, which reached approximately R$18 billion.

Sistema S has received public funding since its inception, but in 2008 MEC suggested a series of changes in order to promote more efficient application of these funds. Together with the Ministry of Labor and Employment and the Ministry of Economy, MEC developed an agreement with the industry and commerce confederations, the CNI and CNC, to, among other things, increase the number of free of charge vacancies. They also regulated the course load of selected VET programs and courses as a quality control (Picchetti and Abreu Pessoa 2009). In particular, the Free of Charge VET Vacancies Agreement stated that, starting in 2014, two-thirds of SENAC's and SENAI's compulsory revenues must be allocated to providing free places in programs and courses. The agreement also called for a rising level of commitment to implement these changes gradually over a period of five years, from 2009 through 2014, beginning with the reallocation of 20 percent of SENAC's resources and 50 percent of SENAI's resources in 2009 toward complying with this new agreement.

Monitoring and Evaluation of Technical and Technological Education

This section briefly describes the monitoring and evaluation (M&E) conducted by the most important providers of technical education, the public network of federal-level and state-level schools and Sistema S.

Brazil's education system has a long history of collecting nationwide data on school and student characteristics and in carrying out student assessments in general subjects. In particular, Brazil has an excellent set administrative data on all its schools (both public and private) that have been captured by its Censo Escolar. Since 1991, the country has been developing nationwide student assessments. Three important administrative data sets for technical education cover students in the public network of federal- and state-level schools and Sistema S: SISTEC; Censo Escolar, and the Sistema de Avaliação da Educação Básica (SAEB, Basic Education Evaluation System and ENEM student assessments. All three sets of data are systematically collected and administered by MEC and the Instituto Nacional de Estudos e Pesquisas (INEP, National Institute of Studies and Research).

Although this information is collected regularly, it is seldom used to adequately inform policy in technical education, including decisions on the allocations of resources to the providers that are most effective in delivering relevant and good-quality education to students. Only such allocations would give providers the incentives needed to improve performance. In particular, the adequacy of the assessments of technical degrees, a more thorough tracking of students over time and into the labor market, and the use of information to reward the performance of providers, schools, and teachers form two of recommendations for improving Brazil's system of M&E for technical education, which is discussed shortly.

Sistema Nacional de Informações da Educação Profissional e Tecnológica (SISTEC)

SISTEC is an online tool used to collect information on any institution that offers technical education at the secondary level. In addition to information on technical courses, it collects information on the FIC courses offered by providers of technical courses. However, SISTEC only gathers information on students in FIC courses when these courses are provided by institutions that also offer technical courses. This implies that if an institution only offers FICs or even technological education at the tertiary level, their courses and students are not included in SISTEC. The system collects for each school the courses provided and some administrative information about both courses and students (Each school must register all new students on a monthly basis.) SISTEC also collects information on whether the course taken by a student is free of charge; if the student has self-declared as low-income; and whether the student has received a scholarship. SISTEC does not, however, follow students over time to track transitions into tertiary education or into the labor market. Currently, no other systematic monitoring system in Brazil tracks such information, creating an important gap in valuable information that could be used for policy decisions.

Censo Escolar

Censo Escolar collects yearly administrative data on enrollments and school inputs such as teachers, school revenues, and movement of resources. It is one of the main reference data sets for policy development and implementation in education, including the calculation of education-related public transfers such as FUNDEB. Censo Escolar is coordinated and carried out by INEP-MEC with the collaboration of the state and municipal secretaries of education. It covers all public and private schools that provide basic education in Brazil, including technical education, from preschool through youth and adult education (EJA). Since 2007, the census has also collected individual information on all students and education professionals (including teachers and other school staff). This information frequently helps school directors in monitoring their staffing for each school term. Among other things, the data include information on the educational degrees of teachers and allows directors and school staff to compute retention and dropout rates. The methodology used makes it possible to compare results over time across schools, networks, grades, states, and municipalities.

Student Assessments, ENEM and SAEB

INEP-MEC conducts regular student assessments—SAEB (Sistema Nacional de Avaliação da Educaçao Básica) and ENEM (Exame Nacional do Ensino Médio)—that could be informative for the monitoring of technical courses at the upper secondary level. SAEB was designed to collect data to evaluate the basic education system. It examines secondary school student performances in

Portuguese and math. It also collects data on the socioeconomic characteristics of students taking the exam and demographic data, professional profiles, and working conditions of teachers and school principals. SAEB covers primary education and students at the 3rd grade of *ensino medio* regular, but not all classes and students at that grade participate. The sample of schools and classes that participate is representative of the public and private network across the country. SAEB is not ideal for looking at student performance in technical courses because it does not include a representative sample of technical schools nationwide.

ENEM is a nonmandatory national exam that evaluates upper secondary education (high school) in Brazil. The student score is typically used for the certification of completion of upper secondary, as well as an entrance/qualification exam to enter higher education or apply for a scholarship in private universities. The test is also used for selection into Programa Universidade para Todos (ProUni, University Program for All), a MEC program that provides scholarships for qualified students. Since 2009, ENEM has been used both as an admissions test to enroll in 23 federal universities and 26 educational institutes and as a certification for a high school degree in youth and adult education. Indeed, it has been growing in importance for students who want to attend university. Both SAEB and ENEM, however, measure only general subjects and not technical ones. Technical students in integrado, ioncomitante, or subsequente modalities, similar to those who complete only the traditional academic upper secondary track, can register for ENEM. Nevertheless, ENEM continues to be a noncompulsory exam that does not assess technical subjects. Making ENEM a mandatory nationwide exam at the end of secondary education would expand its coverage to all technical education students in upper secondary and assess, at a minimum, student performance in general nontechnical subjects. This is one potential avenue for improving M&E of technical education.

Federal Network of VET

The federal network of VET collects administrative data on all students enrolled in the network. These data and administrative records are used to monitor attendance and the repetition and dropout rates of students in the network. Information gathered on the federal network helps to complete that collected by the Censo Escolar and SISTEC at the secondary level, where information on the federal network of VET is still lacking. Labor market outcomes from technical education in the federal network are also not systematically measured. Occasionally, former students are followed anecdotally through informal feedback from a nonrandom sample of graduates.

Table 2.3 summarizes the existing M&E structure for technical education in the three main areas of M&E: (1) monitoring current students, (2) the learning evaluation system, and (2) tracking students' transition to and performance in the labor market.

Table 2.3 Monitoring Systems for Technical Education by Type of Provider: Brazil, 2007

		Monitoring and Evaluation System		
		Monitoring students	Learning Evaluation System	Evaluation of Performance in the labor market
Public Systems	Federal Institutes	Censo Escolar/Inep and Sistec / Setec	ENEM (general subjects)	Not systematic but they keep in contact with graduated students anecdotally
	State schools	Censo Escolar/Inep and Sistec / Setec	ENEM (general subjects)	Not systematic
Sistema S	SENAI/SP	Censo Escolar/Inep and Sistec / Setec	ENEM (general subjects)	A survey is done with graduated students and with industry employers anecdotally
	SENAC/SP	Censo Escolar/Inep and Sistec / Setec		A survey is done and they keep in contact with graduated students and with employers.

Source: Based on MEC (2007) and interviews with representatives from each provider in the public systems and Sistema S cited.
Note: SENAI/SP = Serviço Nacional de Aprendizagem Industrial (National Service of Industrial Learning)/São Paulo; SENAC/SP = Serviço Nacional de Aprendizagem Comercial (National Commercial Training Service)/São Paulo; ENEM = Exame Nacional do Ensino Médio (National High School Exam); INEP = Instituto Nacional de Estudos e Pesquisas (INEP, National Institute of Studies and Research); Sistema Nacional de Informações da Educação Profissional e Tecnológica (SISTEC, National System of Professional and Technological Education); Secretaria de Educação Profissional e Tecnológica (SETEC, Office of Vocational and Technological Education).

Expanding VET with the National Technical Education and Employment Program (PRONATEC)

In Brazil, vocational and technical education and training have experienced important growth over the last several years, and the effort continues to progress today. From 2007 to 2011 alone, enrollment in technical education (at the secondary level) grew by 60 percent, from 780,000 to 1.25 million students. Meanwhile, a new Projeto de Lei do Plano Nacional de Educação (PNL, National Education Plan Project) established 20 goals to be achieved by the Brazilian education system over the next 10 years.[18] Of these, two goals explicitly concern VET: (1) enrollments in vocational programs for youth and adult vocational courses (relative to all education enrollments for youth and adults) should increase from the current 1.5 percent of total enrollments to 25 percent; and (2) enrollments in technical courses (at the secondary level) should be three times their current level. This implies a target of approximately 3.75 million openings—or vacancies—by 2024 for new students in technical education. With this expansionary objective, the federal government created PRONATEC in 2011.

PRONATEC is a set of policies intended to coordinate and promote the expansion of VET in Brazil. It has additional new resources that will be used to expand all modalities of VET, with some targeting of specific groups such as beneficiaries of cash transfer programs, the unemployed, and public schools students. The next section describes PRONATEC's core features and principal challenges.

Design Features of PRONATEC

Under PRONATEC, an umbrella program, MEC coordinates and organizes the set of policies that address vocational and technical education and training programs. PRONATEC's primary objectives are to (1) expand the supply of vocational education, including the construction, reform, and expansion of the state-level network of vocational and technical education as well as the federal network; (2) increase workers' educational opportunities from initial training to professional qualification; (3) increase the quantity of pedagogical resources to support the supply of vocational education; and (4) improve the quality of secondary education.

As an umbrella program, PRONATEC also integrates the three major networks of vocational education provision: federal level, state level, and Sistema S. Some of the policies that fall under PRONATEC already existed before 2011 such as Bolsa Formação, Brasil Profissionalizado (Brazil Professionalized), and expansion of the federal VET system, while others are new initiatives such as the Free of Charge VET Vacancies Agreement between MEC and Sistema S and E-TEC). Under this new arrangement, all federal initiatives regarding VET are coordinated by MEC. Although PRONATEC is a federal program, states also participate in it as administrators of the federal subsidy programs under PRONATEC such as Brasil Profissionalizado, Bolsa Formação, and Bolsa Formação Trabalhador. State governments are also responsible for disseminating information about PRONATEC to their municipalities and helping them to access the benefits of the program.

Similar to the typology of existing VET programs, PRONATEC proposes a dual system of education provision—long-duration programs (PRONATEC-TEC) aimed at the secondary school–age population and shorter-duration programs (PRONATEC-FIC) aimed at the population that is already out of school (either unemployed or working). PRONATEC-TEC is designed, in particular, to promote the concomitante modality in which an improved general secondary curriculum was designed to develop strong math, literacy, foreign language, and critical thinking skills. PRONATEC, however, can be better understood by taking a closer look at the program's principal objectives, the programs housed under PRONATEC, its beneficiaries, and the flow of funds through PRONATEC. The sections that follow will also identify some of the main challenges facing PRONATEC.[19]

Objectives of PRONATEC

PRONATEC was developed to support the rapid expansion of existing VET networks, while facilitating access to vocational education courses. This is happening in alternative but complementary ways. First, PRONATEC will promote the expansion of the federal network of VET providers, including the Federal Institutes for Professional Education in Science and Technology. Through 2014, PRONATEC will also finance and coordinate the construction of 208 new schools, which will create 600,000 openings for students.

Second, PRONATEC will promote expansion of the state network of VET providers through the program Brasil Profissionalizado. This arm of the program aims to strengthen and integrate technical and academic education at the secondary level into state networks. This expansion will take place in partnership with the federal government by channeling federal funding to the states for infrastructure, teacher training, and developing management capacity and pedagogical practices.

Third, PRONATEC will expand the e-learning network through E-Tec Brasil, which offers free distance learning FIC courses and technical education programs as well as professional qualification programs (that is, training programs). The e-learning network currently offers courses through the Federal Network of Institutes of Professional Education in Science and Technology, through Sistema S, and through professional education institutions linked to state education systems.

Fourth, PRONATEC oversees the Free of Charge VET Vacancies Agreement between MEC and Sistema S (Acordo de Gratuidade). The objective of this agreement is to progressively expand the free of charge VET openings offered by Sistema S to low-income Brazilians. By 2014 two-thirds of the revenue from mandatory contributions imposed on payrolls, which fund Sistema S, must be applied to the provision of a free VET education.

Fifth, PRONATEC will expand financing for education through the FIES-TEC Fund for Financing Technical Education for Students. This program provides financing for students who do not qualify for one of the many free beneficiary programs, but who are enrolled or wish to enroll in technical education or FIC courses in private institutions or Sistema S. FIES also provides financing for firms to provide training and professional qualification for their employees.

Finally, PRONATEC has created a new program, Bolsa-Formação, through which it offers free technical education courses for low-income students enrolled in public secondary education as well as FIC courses for vulnerable social groups. Although publicly provided technical education is already free, those enrolled through Bolsa-Formação also receive financial support for course materials, transportation, and meals. Students subsidized by Bolsa-Formação can take courses offered through federal and state secondary schools and through Sistema S.

Beneficiaries of PRONATEC

PRONATEC's beneficiaries are primarily students enrolled in secondary education, workers, and unemployed or inactive individuals from the most vulnerable groups. In fact, a large part of PRONATEC's initiatives are focused on ensuring that the expansion of VET reaches the poor and vulnerable populations of the country. The demand for courses offered through PRONATEC arises directly from these beneficiaries. Students in secondary education may enroll directly in courses through their local secondary schools or vocational education institutions.

Several federal ministries, however, also create demand by partnering with PRONATEC to provide courses that meet a sector's needs for specific human capital. For example, the Ministry of Tourism launched the PRONATEC Copa campaign targeting companies in the tourism industry to raise awareness of free tourism-related courses for their employees. These courses were sponsored by PRONATEC and the Ministry of Tourism in preparation for the 2014 World Cup in Brazil. Similarly, the Ministry of Communications has partnered with PRONATEC to provide vocational education courses in order to train 76,000 telecom technicians in an effort to increase the supply and qualifications of the labor force for this sector. Figure 2.7, illustrates the different flows from beneficiaries to providers and the types of vocational and technical education offered.

Implementation of PRONATEC

Implementation of PRONATEC's initiatives depends on the partner. Generally, federal-level initiatives are implemented by MEC, while programs providing support to state-level institutes or networks are implemented by states and municipalities. This section describes some examples of the implementation arrangements under PRONATEC, particularly the Free of Charge VET Vacancies Agreement, Brasil Professionalizado, Bolsa Formação, and Brasil Sem Miseria (Brazil without Extreme Poverty).

Figure 2.7 PRONATEC: Program Beneficiaries and Providers

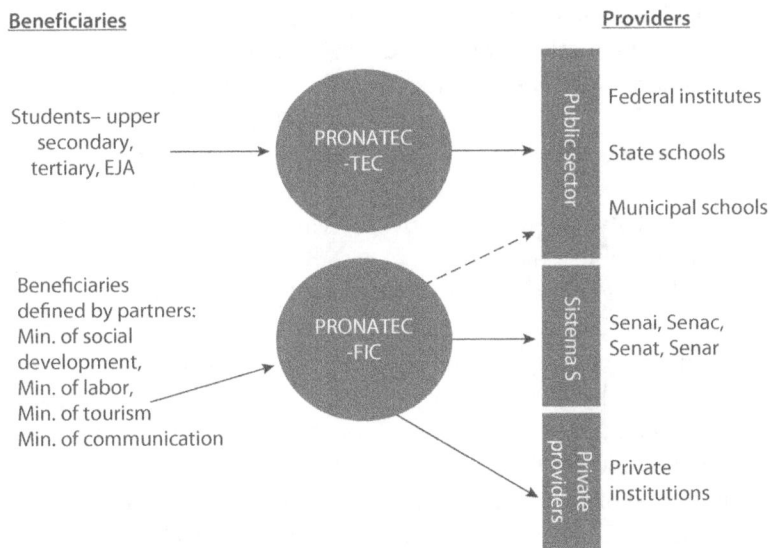

Source: Created by the Authors, based on information provided by MEC.
Note: PRONATEC = Programa Nacional de Acesso ao Ensino Técnico e Emprego (National Program for Access to Technical Education and Employment); EJA = educação jovens e adultos (youth and adult education); SENAI = Serviço Nacional de Aprendizagem Industrial (National Service of Industrial Learning); SENAC = Serviço Nacional de Aprendizagem Comercial (National Commercial Training Service); SENAT = Serviço Nacional de Aprendizagem do Transporte (National Transportation Learning Service); SENAR = Serviço Nacional de Aprendizagem Rural (National Rural Education Service); FIC = curso de formação inicial e continuada (initial and continuing training course).

The expansion of the federal VET supply through the Federal Institutes is the responsibility of MEC. However, implementation of the Free of Charge VET Vacancies Agreement signed between MEC and Sistema S is the responsibility of Sistema S and is monitored by MEC. Other programs, however, are driven and supported by MEC and carried out by partners.

The participation of the state-level education systems in Brasil Profissionalizado is largely carried out by the counterparts in the state government responsible for technical education. To qualify, a state secretariat has to be a signatory of the commitment "All in Favor of Education" (Todos pela Educação)[20] and has to accept MEC guidance in the diagnosis of the state's particular education needs and in the preparation of a plan to improve VET.[21] The resulting diagnostic report and plan must be submitted to MEC. If approved, a covenant may be signed, allowing the state government to receive support through Brasil Professionalizado.

Municipalities can also participate in Bolsa Formação. Municipalities, usually represented by the secretariat of education, labor, or social development, can join PRONATEC through a MEC website. Courses are then offered by authorized providers in the area, usually Federal Institutes and Sistema S. The municipal representatives are responsible for negotiating with providers on which courses will be offered in each case and for disseminating information on the VET courses and programs available through Bolsa Formação among the potential beneficiaries. These beneficiaries, however, also have to preregister through the PRONATEC website. Municipal representatives are responsible for monitoring the courses and organizing the graduation ceremony upon completion of a VET program. Municipal representatives also provide ongoing support for the beneficiaries as well as promote policies with a focus on the labor market.

The Pronatec–Brasil Sem Miséria partnership allows those who receive social assistance benefits from the Ministry of Social Development, Ministry of Labor and Employment, and state and municipal departments of social assistance (such as Bolsa Família recipients) to have priority access to the Bolsa Formação Trabalhador courses (see table 2.4).

Table 2.4 reports the target enrollments nationwide for PRONATEC between 2011 and 2014. As of May 2012, PRONATEC had served around over 2.5 million Brazilians and aimed to expand vacancies in short courses (FICs) and technical programs to 8 million by 2014. As of mid-2014, PRONATEC had served approximately 7.27 million, close to meeting its goal of 8 million. In addition, the federal government announced a second phase of PRONATEC that will build on the first phase with a goal of enrolling 12 million students in technical education and vocational training (in 220 TEC courses and 640 FIC courses) between 2015 and 2018.

Financial resources for PRONATEC are mainly provided by MEC's budget, the Fundo de Apoio Trabalhador (FAT, Fund for Worker Support), the integrated Social Action System, Sistema S, and the Banco Nacional de Desenvolvimento Econômico e Social (BNDES, Brazilian Development Bank)—see figure 2.8.

Table 2.4 PRONATEC Targets for Enrollment by Policy: Brazil, 2011–14

Cursos técnicos	2011	2012	2013	2014	Total 2011–2014
Total Bolsa Formação Estudante	9.415	99.149	151.313	151.313	411.190
Brasil Profissionalizado	33.295	90.563	172.321	233.781	529.960
E-TEC Brasil	74.000	150.000	200.000	250.000	674.000
Continuidade do Acordo Sistema S	56.416	76.119	110.545	161.389	404.469
Total Rede Federal de EPCT	72.000	79.560	90.360	101.160	343.080
Total	**245.126**	**495.391**	**724.539**	**897.643**	**2.362.699**
Cursos fic	2011	2012	2013	2014	Total 2011–2014
Total Bolsa Formação Trabalhador	226.421	590.937	743.717	1.013.027	2.574.102
Continuidade do Acordo Sistema S	421.723	570.020	821.965	1.194.266	3.007.974
Total	**684.144**	**1.160.957**	**1.565.682**	**2.207.293**	**5.582.076**
Total	**893.270**	**1.656.348**	**2.290.221**	**3.104.936**	**7.944.775**

Source: Secretaria de Educação Profissional e Tecnológica (SETEC, Office of Vocational and Technological Education)–Ministério da Educação (MEC, Ministry of Education) 2012.

Figure 2.8 PRONATEC Funding Flow, 2011–14

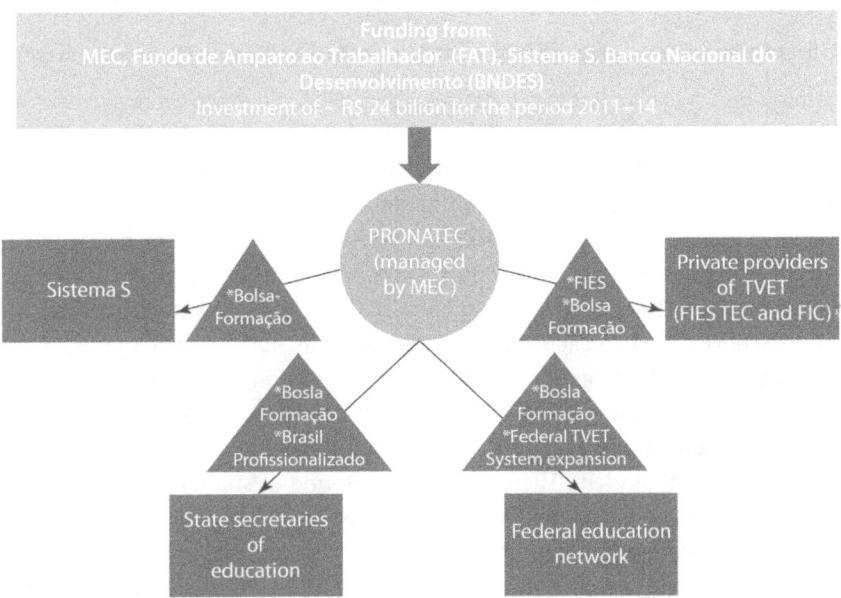

Sources: Ministério da Educação (MEC, Ministry of Education), http://www.mec.gov.br/; Programa Nacional de Acesso ao Ensino Técnico e Emprego (PRONATEC, National Program for Access to Technical Education and Employment), http://pronatec.mec.gov.br/.
Note: FAT = Fundo de Apoio Trabalhador (Fund for Worker Support); SENAI = Serviço Nacional de Aprendizagem Industrial (National Service of Industrial Learning); BNDES = Banco Nacional de Desenvolvimento Econômico e Social (Brazilian Development Bank); VET = vocational and education and training; FIES = Fundo de Financiamento ao Estudante do Ensino Técnico(Fund for Financing Technical Education for Students); FIC = cursos de formação inicial e continuada (initial and continuing training courses).

Funds are channeled through the Sistema S national network of secondary-level technical schools and through federal and state/municipal vocational education networks to provide Bolsa Formação courses that are free of charge for the student, and are channeled to other projects that expand access to vocational education such as infrastructure and teacher training.

Although VET traditionally has been the responsibility of Federal Institutes or of private providers, more recently some states have invested more in technical education as part of their mandate to provide secondary education. At the state level, provision usually involves technical education combined with the completion of academic secondary education. For example, well before PRONATEC the states of São Paulo and Minas Gerais developed their own state-level technical and vocational education and training programs. Box 2.2 describes these experiences that preceded PRONATEC at the state level. São Paulo's Vence program and Minas Gerais's Rede de Formação Profissional Orientada pelo Mercado and Programa de Ensino Profissionalizante (Network of Market-Oriented Professional Training and the Program for Professional Education) are three state-level experiences in providing technical education. The programs were created with the objective of promoting a better alignment between the skills being produced for the labor market and the needs of the private sector.

Box 2.2 Expanding State-Level VET: The Experiences of São Paulo and Minas Gerais

The Secretaria de Estado da Educação de São Paulo (SEE, São Paulo State secretary of education) created Vence using two different models. Vence Integrado provides a new curriculum combining regular academic programs and technical programs. Students who join a school sign up for one program that includes both academic and technical subjects. In this model, SEE has two (public) partners: the Instituto Federal de São Paulo (São Paulo Federal Institute) and Centro Paula Souza. Both institutions collaborate to develop the new curricula and teach in conjunction. In 2013, 2,500 new openings were offered through Vence across 74 São Paulo secondary schools. In the second model, Vence Concomitante, students in lower or upper secondary education can apply to a technical program in a private institute while they finalize their general academic secondary education. Private institutes are selected through a public procurement process and receive a monetary transfer per student. There is strict monitoring of student attendance and supervision of course quality. Payment to the private institution is made only for students who are attending classes regularly and is conditional on student performance to ensure provider accountability and that learning occurs. As of mid-2013, Vence Concomitante had reached over 50,000 students, who could choose among 56 VET programs offered by 174 providers.

Rede de Formação Profissional Orientada pelo Mercado is managed by the Minas Gerais Secretariat of Science, Technology, and Tertiary Education. The program currently has 84 centros vocacionais tecnológicos (CVTs, technological vocational centers) and 487 telecentros,

box continues next page

Box 2.2 Expanding State-Level VET: The Experiences of São Paulo and Minas Gerais *(continued)*

which reach more than 360 municipalities in the state. It also provides free Internet access. The CVTs offer courses in many fields and graduate technicians in strategic areas for each region of the state. They also support new entrepreneurs to stimulate local innovation. By 2009, R$130 million had been invested, 500,000 citizens had been certified, and 1 billion people had benefited from free Internet access.

The professional development program (Programa de Ensino Profissionalizante) was launched in Minas Gerais in 2007 as a voucher program to diversify and expand the technical and vocational training options for youth and young adults. The state pays the tuition for students to attend any state-accredited training program, whether offered by a private school, municipal school, or industry-based center. The courses are typically 14–24 months long and often organized in partnership with employers to guarantee the relevance of the skills being taught. Many of these partners have also committed to hiring graduates. By 2010, 158,000 students had applied for the 28,000 openings. A key factor in this program's success is that schools have an incentive to help students stay in school and succeed academically; the state secretariat transfers voucher payments to the institutions every two months based on an audit of the number of students enrolled and their attendance records.

Sources: Secretaria de *Estado da* Educação *de* São Paulo (*SEE, São Paulo State secretary of education*); Inclusão Digital; World Bank 2012.

Notes

1. See Instituto Nacional de Estudos e Pesquisas (INEP, National Institute of Studies and Research), 2013, http://www.inep.gov.br/.
2. Officials from Sistema S noted in interviews conducted for this report that distance education is often considered less prestigious than face-to-face modalities of education delivery. This, then, is an additional challenge to the growth of distance learning. Moreover, issues of connectivity and the reliability of electricity (particularly in rural locations with outdated electrical wiring) can present infrastructure challenges that limit the access and effectiveness of distance education.
3. See Lei No. 10.097/2000 and Decreto No. 5.598/2005, Ministry of Labor and Employment.
4. See PNAD 2007.
5. In some data sources, Sistema S is considered a private provider because, although it is funded by public taxes on industry, it has historically offered courses at the request of the private sector (including FICs).
6. The topic of FICS, or short-duration training programs, is revisited in Gukovas et al. (2013).
7. The information presented here on SENAI and SENAC was collected from their websites.
8. These methods are not used just for filling no-charge vacancies. SENAI and SENAC also offer for-fee courses, some of which have different eligibility criteria when

companies contract and pay for courses for their employees. In these cases, vacancies are preferentially or exclusively filled at the discretion of the entity contracting the service

9. The Quotas Law (Lei de Cotas) for the federal education network went into effect in 2013.
10. Among other things, the Lei de Diretrizes e Bases da Educação of 1996 requires that all students in secondary school take the same combination of required academic courses. These can be complemented but not replaced by technical education.
11. The 2012 version of the Catálogo Nacional de Cursos Técnico lists 220 programs distributed across 13 technological axes. A list of all courses from the catalogue can be accessed at http://pronatec.mec.gov.br/cnct/.
12. According to Almério Melquíades Araújo, coordinator for upper secondary and technical courses at Centro Paula Souza, experience is usually not a selection criterion. Teachers in the public system are usually approved to begin on the initial step of their career.
13. FUNDEB is funded by 20 percent of each of the following sources of state and municipal revenue: Fundo de Participação dos Estados (FPE, State Participation Fund); Fundo de Participação dos Municípios (FPM, Municipal Participation Fund); Imposto sobre Circulação de Mercadorias e Serviços (ICMS, Tax on Services and Merchandise); Imposto sobre Produtos Industrializados, proporcional às exportações (IPIexp, Tax on Industrial Products proportional to exports); Desoneração das Exportações (LC no. 87/96); Imposto sobre Transmissão Causa Mortis e Doações (ITCMD, Estate and Donations Tax); Imposto sobre Propriedade de Veículos Automotores (IPVA, Motor Vehicle Property Tax); Cota parte de 50 percent do Imposto Territorial Rural-ITR devida aos municípios (50 percent quote on Rural Territories owed to municipalities).
14. For more information about FUNDEB or public financing of education in Brazil, see Ulyssea, Fernandes, and Gremaud (2006).
15. FUNDEB replaced FUNDEF (funding system in force between 1997 and 2006), which was composed of 15 percent of public resources linked by law to education, and it was distributed according to enrollments in primary and lower secondary education. The federal government provided the fund with complementary resources, but these amounted to only 1 percent of the total resource in the last years of FUNDEF.
16. SIOPE is the federal system that collects data on public education spending at the municipal, state, and federal levels.
17. Using PNAD (2007), Vasconcellos, Biondi, and Menezes-Filho (2012) and Almeida et al. (2015) show that over their lifetime, students who complete technical education have on average a 9.7 percent higher salary than those who only complete academic upper secondary (high school equivalent). This figure yields an internal rate of return for public investment per student in technical education of 14 percent per year. In addition, the studies note that this benefit comes at an additional per student cost of R$2,886 for technical education than for an academic upper secondary education. However, the difference in costs between the two modalities would need to reach at least R$11,500 to make the individual investment in technical education not worthwhile.
18. This law is pending approval by National Congress to become a de facto law.
19. This section draws heavily in information kindly provided by MEC or gathered from the website http://www.pronatec.mec.gov.br.

20. Until 2012, only Federal Institutes and Sistema S were authorized by MEC to be PRONATEC providers for the training scholarship program, Bolsa Formação. Ordinance No. 168 of March 2013 defines new rules, allowing state and municipal systems of VET and private institutions to provide courses funded by PRONATEC-Bolsa-Formação, along with the Federal Institutes and Sistema S.
21. This commitment is regulated by Decreto No. 6.094/2007.

References

Almeida, Rita Kullberg Leandro Anazawa, Naercio Menezes Filho, and Ligia Maria De Vasconcellos. 2015. "Investing in Technical & Vocational Education and Training: Does It Yield Large Economic Returns in Brazil." Policy Research Working Paper; no. WPS 7246, World Bank, Washington, DC http://documents.worldbank.org/curated/en/2015/04/24411547/investing-technical-vocational-education-training-yield-large-economic-returns-brazil.

Gukovas, Renata, Joana Silva, Karla Carolina Marra, and Jociany Monteiro Luz. 2013. *Qualificações e empregos políticas ativas e passivas de mercado de trabalho no Brasil: Estrutura, inovações e oportunidades.* Rio de Janeiro: Ministry of Labor and Employment, Brazil; Washington, DC: World Bank.

MEC (Ministério da Educação). 2007. "Legislação sobre a obrigatoriedade do preenchimento do censo escolar." Portaria do 264.

MEC (Ministério da Educação/Ministry of Education). 2012. Relatório de Gestão da Secretaria de Educação Profissional e Tecnológica: Exercício de 2012. SETEC (Secretaria de Educação Profissional e Tecnológica/Office of Vocational and Technological Education), Brazil.

Neri, Marcelo. 2010. "A Educação Profissional e Você no Mercado de Trabalho." FGV/CPS (Fundação Getulio Vargas/Centro de Políticas Sociais), Rio de Janeiro.

Picchetti, Paulo, and Samuel de Abreu Pessoa. 2009. "Relatório Final de Pesquisa: O Sistema S." IBRE/FGV (Instituto Brasileiro de Economia/ Fundação Getulio Vargas), Rio de Janeiro.

PNAD (Pesquisa Nacional por Amostra de Domicílios/National Household Sample Survey). 2007. IBGE (Instituto Brasileiro de Geografia e Estatistica/Brazilian Insitute for Geography and Statistics), Brazil.

Schwartzman, Simon, and Claudio Moura de Castro. 2013. "Estudo e Trabalho da Juventude Brasileira." Working paper, Instituto de Estudo do Trabalho e Sociedade (IETS), Rio de Janeiro.

SENAC (*Serviço Nacional de Aprendizagem Comercial*—National Service for Commercial Training). 2010. "A Brazilian Institution of Professional/Vocational Education Open to All of Society." http://www.senac.br/.

SENAI (*Serviço Nacional de Aprendizagem Industrial*—National Service of Industrial Learning). 2010. "A Network of Not-for-Profit Secondary Level Professional Schools Established and Maintained by the Brazilian Confederation of Industry (a Patronal Syndicate)." http://www.senaipr.org.br/.

Ulyssea, G., R. Fernandes, and A. P. Gremaud. 2006. O impacto do FUNDEF na alocação de recursos para a educação básica. *Pesquisa e Planejamento Econômico* 36 (1): 109-36.

Vasconcellos, Lígia, Roberta Loboda Biondi, and Naercio Menezes-Filho. 2012. *Enhancing Quality of Education in Latin America: Evaluating the Impact of the Brazilian Public School Mathematics Olympics*. Sao Paulo: Rede de Economia Aplicada (REAP).

World Bank. 2012. "Brazil: Third Minas Gerais Development Partnership DPL." Report No. 62267-BR, World Bank, Washington, DC.

CHAPTER 3

Brazil's VET System: Implementation Challenges, Opportunities, and International Examples

Introduction

This chapter discusses six critical challenges and opportunities for the delivery of technical education at the upper secondary level in Brazil and presents relevant international examples and good practices: (1) aligning the skills provided by vocational and technical education and training (VET) courses with the needs of the labor market demand and ensuring workplace learning; (2) improving and expanding the monitoring and evaluation of VET; (3) improving the dissemination of information available to students, especially for choosing a career and education path; (4) raising the quality and relevance of the VET system by better preparing teachers; (5) identifying alternative ways of promoting innovation in the VET system as a way to boost competitiveness and productivity; and (6) expanding VET to reach the most vulnerable.

Aligning Skills Provided by the VET System with the Needs of the Labor Market

Promoting a Good Match between the Supply and Demand of Skills

In Brazil, VET providers may offer any course that is part of the Catálogo Nacional de Cursos Técnicos (National Catalogue of Technical Education). Providers such as the Centro Paula Souza in São Paulo and Serviço Nacional de Aprendizagem Comercial (SENAC, National Commercial Training Service) affirm that the methodologies used to define the courses that are offered in a particular institution tend to be similar. When a new school or new program is created, providers, whether private or public, typically conduct market research in conjunction with local employers and markets to identify and select the courses that best fit local needs. Representatives of employers who have encountered difficulties in hiring qualified employees for specific functions may also directly seek providers' help. Together, the VET providers and the employers plan the appropriate way to train and supply the numbers of people with the qualifications sought.

Internationally, meeting labor market demands with VET has been a challenge for many countries in both the developing and developed worlds. However, a number of good practices have emerged from countries' experiences in finding a balance between providing youth with transferable skills that support occupational mobility and lifelong learning and providing them with occupationally specific skills that meet the labor market's immediate needs (OECD 2011).

To this end, employers and unions need to be engaged in curriculum development, sharing inputs and apprenticeship opportunities to ensure that the skills taught correspond to those needed in a modern workplace. Providing this mix may also require engaging employers, unions, and other stakeholders to develop and implement qualification frameworks and standardized national assessments frameworks to ensure the quality and consistency of teaching and training. It is important to note, however, that adequate numeracy and literacy skills, which support lifelong learning and career development, are indispensable foundations. Any weaknesses in these areas should be identified and addressed within vocational programs.

Box 3.1 briefly describes Chile's approach to overcoming schools' lack of information about which occupations should each year receive more attention in training students. This experience from the mining sector is one example of a market-oriented, sector-based approach to identifying and mitigating skills gaps. In Chile, industry or sector skills councils meet on a regular basis to discuss strategic and short- and long-run gaps. This information is made available to the public, and, with the support of skills accreditation and providers' certification, the market clears with success. The scheme, however, is relatively light on government intervention, with most of the public support focused on ensuring coordination and providing the right regulatory framework.[1]

For industries that share similar characteristics (for example, a small number of large firms) and in which the incentives to coordinate are high (such as aviation, mining, and oil and gas operations), Brazil could look to developing a similar set of sector skills councils, particularly at the state level, inviting local representatives of sectors to offer their perspectives on the occupations and professions most in demand. However, there is no one-size-fits-all model. For example, for industries with a high number of small and medium enterprises (SMEs), the transaction costs of such a structure might be too large, and a different approach may be needed. Recent research undertaken by the Organisation for Economic Co-operation and Development (OECD) highlights the importance of decentralized and demand-driven skills development for SMEs. This often takes the form of regionally based networks and skills ecosystems that include partnerships between local education and training intuitions and SMEs organized around the principle of workforce development. Here the government

Box 3.1 Developing an Education and Training System for the Mining Sector in Chile

Mining is one of Chile's largest sectors and a major driver of the economy. From 2012 to 2015, skills gaps and shortages were one of the most important challenges for development of the sector. Attraction rates for mining-related VET were at a low of 1.45 percent, and the completion rate for mining-related VET was only 21 percent. Thus two important challenges were how to increase retention and the completion rates of students in VET and how to attract more students.

The various studies undertaken by the mining sector skills council (which included representatives of mining companies, contractors, training providers, and government) resulted in the development of a sector strategy. In the short run, it aims at bridging the 2012–15 skills shortage and in the long run at installing the capacity to ensure the quantity and quality of human resources and guarantee the sector's sustainability and growth. The sector strategy includes program accreditation standards and job competency certification and a technical and professional qualifications framework; the design and implementation of an attraction strategy; fast-track training and retraining programs (minimum of 400 hours) for entry-level technicians (18,900 operators and 8,708 maintenance workers); and improvements in Chile's overall capacity for delivering VET by means of investment projects that establish state-of-the-art training hubs in regions lacking a sufficient supply of VET.

Although the outcomes of this strategy are still in the making, the speed at which this partnership of public, private, and academic stakeholders has mobilized resources and begun to implement this strategy is noteworthy. A first six-month skills gap study in July 2011 resulted in the Ministry of Labor's approval of devoting US$15 billion to train workers for entry-level and maintenance occupations in May 2012, the September 2012 launch of a mining industry skills council, the appointment of Fundación Chile to coordinate implementation, and the completion of a second version of the skills gap study with updated data that same month. This result demonstrates the potential effectiveness of sector skills councils in engaging employers to better allow VET to meet labor market demand.

Source: Araneda 2013.

---

has an important role to play in providing infrastructure and resources for the development of these networks, as well as evidence about the returns to investment in skills and about the impacts of policy interventions as an incentive for SMEs to participate in these types of initiatives (for a discussion, see Almeida, Behrman, and Robalino 2011).

Moreover, Brazil shares similarities with countries such as Australia, where the economy operates at different "speeds" in different industries and regions and is affected by a federalized system. Brazil could examine the pros and cons of Australia's experience in developing a set of 11 industry skills councils, which have had a central role in building and maintaining Australia's National Occupations Standards and in driving vocational training. It could also look more closely at other countries and regions with devolved governments that have adopted a sector skills approach such as India, the United Kingdom, Canada, and the European Union (OECD 2013).

Ensuring Workplace Learning

Many technical programs in Brazil still do not require apprenticeships or other types of workplace learning as part of the curriculum. In addition, the trend seems to be one of moving away from making this learning modality a standard component of a VET program. Recently, several institutions within Sistema S removed the apprenticeship as a required component of technical education. The decision was made in recognition that, in practice, it is difficult to have a sufficient number of institutions that can offer an apprenticeship to each and every VET student. When considering VET at the secondary school level, however, workplace learning stands out as one of the best ways to promote VET learning that is aligned with the needs of the labor market as well as to build and strengthen socioemotional skills.

Workplace learning serves a number of functions for the student, but also for the employer and the VET system as a whole. For the student, workplace learning provides a strong learning environment because it offers real on-the-job training experience that makes it easier to acquire hard and soft skills. Workplace learning also facilitates a two-way flow of information between potential employers and employees, making recruitment more effective or less costly for the employer. In addition, employer willingness to offer workplace training is a signal and verification that a VET program has labor market value. Because skills forecasts are often difficult to produce with rigor, countries should seek to build VET systems that are driven by student demand and balanced by employer willingness to offer workplace learning and training opportunities (OECD 2010).

In Brazil, the lack of workplace learning as a standard part of technical education programs is partly a result of the difficulty in engaging employers in providing these opportunities. Some states such as Ceará have implemented joint programs with local industry to provide paid internships for graduates, but this is not yet a uniform practice, nor is it fully integrated into a VET curriculum.[2] By law, there is still no de facto obligation on the part of VET providers to offer apprenticeships or other forms of workplace learning for technical education, although the Catologo Nacional de Cursos Tecnicos indicates that apprenticeships and workplace learning can be carried out in addition to the required minimum number of hours in the classroom for technical education and not in place of this classroom time. From the perspective of employers, the Lei de Aprendizagem of 2000 does legally mandate that in all medium and large firms 5–15 percent of the professional employees must be students, but these opportunities are neither exclusive to technical education students nor available in all regions and municipalities and sectors.

In practice, providing apprenticeships opportunities in all technical education programs in Brazil is further complicated by the inability of certain programs to offer apprenticeships in areas where an industry is weak or nonexistent.

Organizations such as the Centro de Integração Empresa-Escola (CIEE, Center for School-Workplace Integration) play an important role in facilitating apprenticeships and matching students with workplace learning opportunities.[3] Nevertheless, CIEE still encounters difficulties in making these matches, especially in the more remote regions of Brazil. In these regions, the type of technical programs offered are typically only those in which there is a market demanding technicians for that particular field. However, the lack of variety of technical programs constrains options for students who have little ability to migrate to other cities or regions. Balancing the existing labor market demand with the need in these regions and municipalities for greater economic development may also be a relevant consideration. Under some circumstances, there may be a need for public policies that intervene both in the demand and supply side, subsidizing job creation and opportunities for students to complete apprenticeships in specific technical fields currently with low demand.[4] To be sure, any such policy should be carried out as part of a larger sectoral strategy that also includes coordination among employers, local governments, and other stakeholders to facilitate such opportunities and ensure they are mutually beneficial.

Internationally, apprenticeships and workplace learning follow different patterns, ranging from apprentices attending school one or two days a week to a sequence of segments with two years of school followed by two years of training. Box 3.2 highlights some of the variety in apprenticeship systems in other countries. These may serve as references as Brazil considers expanding and strengthening opportunities for workplace learning for technical education students.

Box 3.2 International Examples of Workplace Learning

The traditional apprenticeship systems—even the most successful such as the German "dual model"—have been in decline, and yet workplace learning remains a critical component of technical education. Many countries are developing hybrid apprenticeship models to ensure that vocational and technical education students have opportunities to incorporate hands-on experience into their learning. Some of these new models include intercompany training partnerships, modularized apprenticeship systems, cooperative education programs (school-organized but in partnership with companies), and career academies (learning communities in upper secondary schools combining academic and vocational curricula around common themes such as health, technology, and business). Several countries such as Germany, Norway, and the United States provide different examples of workplace learning models.

German GOLO Project. The GOLO Project is an example of an SME learning workplace partnership with rotation or exchange of apprentices among companies. The pilot scheme revolved around a learning workplace partnership to improve the quality of education and training, create new training places, and focus on the needs of SMEs, which often do not have the resources to hire apprentices (Stach and Stöger 2009).

box continues next page

Box 3.2 International Examples of Workplace Learning *(continued)*

Norway's 2+2 System. Norway's traditional 2+2 model consists of two years of apprenticeship in a company, followed by two years in school. The two-year apprenticeship with employers is based on a national curriculum. Legally, apprentices are employees of the enterprise, with conditions specified in a contract, signed by the student, the company and the local government. Apprentices receive a wage that is 30–80 percent of the wage of a qualified worker. Likewise, employers taking on apprentices receive direct subsidies from the local government to cover their training time during the two years of the apprenticeship. Training offices, often owned by companies in a specific industry, work actively to identify new training companies and open new apprenticeships, supervise companies, and train staff involved in the tutoring of apprentices. Norway's system benefits from a well-developed institutional framework that allows for a social partner's involvement in the provision of apprenticeship opportunities and placement of students. This model is, however, better suited for urban settings where distances between home, school, and the workplace are relatively small (Kuczera et al. 2008).

U.S. career academies. Career academies are small learning communities of approximately 150–200 students, often in low-income high schools, combining academic and technical or career curricula and offering workplace opportunities through partnership with local employers. Academies typically focus on a specific field (such as health care). Applicants enter an academy in the first years of upper secondary education (9th or 10th grade). Evaluations have shown that participating young men earn 11–17 percent more a year than nonparticipating students, and gains are sustained after high school graduation. These evaluations also demonstrate the feasibility of improving labor market preparation and successful school-to-work transitions without compromising academic goals and preparation for higher education (Kemple 2008).

Sources: Nam (2009); Stach and Stöger (2009); Kuczera et al. (2008); Kemple (2008).

Monitoring and Evaluation of the VET System

Strengthening the Foundations of M&E: Data Collection and Rigorous Evaluation

Policy makers in Brazil have significant leeway to improve the management of the VET system by promoting a more systematic measurement of results and feedback to inform policy implementation. As illustrated in table 3.1, none of the institutions involved in M&E of VET systematically monitor the placement of students in the labor market or their progression to other or higher levels of education. This type of tracking could be carried out by resorting to administrative data sets or through surveys that systematically measure insertion into the labor market in the short and medium term. It is striking, for example, that no VET institution regularly tracks students using the Relação Anual de Informações Sociais (RAIS, Annual Social Information) administrative data set. Furthermore, detailed information on the technical courses completed by students is not systematically collected in labor force surveys such as the Pesquisa Nacional por Amostra de Domicílios (PNAD, Household Sample National Survey) thereby

Table 3.1 Categories and Types of Indicators Used in VET Evaluation, 2012

Area	Indicators and data availability			
	Data readily available	Data not readily available	Data often not available	
1. Financing	1.1 Spending on formal VET	1.2 Total VET spending by student	1.3 Share of companies providing apprenticeship and other types of training (by size of company)	
			1.4 Share of apprenticeship and other types of training spending in labor cost (by size of company)	
2. Access	2.1 Enrollment in vocational education as a percentage of total enrollment in the formal education system	2.6 Typology of admission policies to formal school-based VET	2.3 Work-based learning participation rate	
		2.7 Transition paths from upper secondary VET education	2.4 Equity	
	2.2 Enrollment by type of VET program		2.5 Unsatisfied demand for VET	
			2.8 Policies on articulation with schooling/higher education	
3. Quality and innovation	3.1 Student to teacher ratio in formal VET and general programs	3.3 Share of apprentices completing registered programs as a percentage of all apprentices starting registered programs	3.5 Relevance of quality assurance systems for VET providers	
	3.2 Completion rate in VET programs and general programs		3.6 Investment in training of teachers and trainers	
			3.7 Utilization of acquired skills in the workplace	
		3.4 Share of qualified teachers in VET and general programs	3.8 Share of information and communication technology training activities in VET	
			3.9 Satisfaction of employers with VET graduates	
4. Relevance	4.1 Employment to population ratio	4.7 Informal employment rate	4.9 Working poverty rate	
	4.2 Unemployment rate	4.8 Time-related unemployment rate	4.10 Average real earnings	
	4.3 Employment status		4.11 Number of vacant jobs	
	4.4 Employment by economic sector		4.12 Net job creation	
	4.5 Employment by occupation		4.13 Youth outside labor force	
	4.6 Literacy rate		4.14 Discouraged workers	

Source: ILO-EFT-UNESCO 2012.
Note: VET = vocational and technical education and training.

creating obstacles to the comparison of different returns. This emerges as significant gap in the VET M&E system, which otherwise seems to be based on a very solid set of databases.

In addition, a review of the existing literature concludes that almost no studies have conducted rigorous evaluations of the effectiveness of VET versus general secondary education tracks. The few exceptions used a special survey covering VET in the 2007 PNAD, which is collected by the Instituto Brasileiro de Geografia e Estatística (IBGE, Brazilian Institute of Geography and Statistics). Neri (2010), Vasconcellos et al. (2010), and Almeida et al. (2015) found that VET positively affects the probability of being employed and is associated with higher income by about 9.7 percent. Their studies suggest that there is a positive and statistically significant private return to investment in VET courses when compared to students without a degree in technical or vocational education but with similar characteristics. Because of the lack of time series information and the nonrandom selection of the general and technical tracks, none of these studies could rigorously control for selection or for the (unobservable) individual heterogeneity that may determine the enrollment in VET courses and the labor market outcomes. Furthermore, there are few efforts at the institutional level to publicly disseminate the returns to different occupations and professions. This stands in stark contrast to what other countries in the region and OECD are doing.

To address these gaps in critical information for policy development and successful implementation, Brazil could consider several components of a strong system of monitoring and evaluation. The objective of a strong M&E system in technical education is to ensure and verify that the VET system provides youth with general, transferable skills that will support professional mobility and lifelong learning, as well as provide specific occupational abilities and skills that respond to short-term labor market needs. Because of the complexity of the Brazilian VET system in terms of the number and types of both providers and programs, a strong M&E system is even more critical to ensuring that technical education meets this overarching goal as effectively, efficiently, and equitably as possible. Moreover, global trends have placed an ever-stronger emphasis on evidence-based policy making, in which policy design is supported by empirical evidence and the use of robust evaluation techniques to evaluate the impacts of programs.

A strong M&E system should in general include components that can help in decision making and alert administrators about existing and potential problems. These components include (1) monitoring the balance between the supply and demand of VET programs and the needs of the economy in the medium and long term; (2) monitoring provider compliance with legal requirements and evaluation of the quality of the VET programs they offer; (3) monitoring student trajectories and employment results; (4) evaluating employer satisfaction with students' education; and (5) evaluating educational outcomes (via standardized national exams in the general education subjects included in technical education). These components can be grouped into distinct but related areas: (1) financing and governance, (2) access and participation, (3) quality and innovation, and (4) relevance, applying a variety of methodologies and a continuous and systematic collection of different types of data. The International Labour Organization, European Training Foundation (EFT), and United Nations Education, Scientific, and Cultural Organization (UNESCO) provide a framework of suggested indicators in these four categories based on the likelihood of data availability, as outlined in table 3.1.

The development of a national strategy for VET research, complemented by a national government–sponsored entity dedicated to the collection of high-quality data and the evaluation of VET, is one approach to consolidating and coordinating the multidisciplinary and multistakeholder endeavor of monitoring and evaluating technical education. Australia's National Centre for Vocational Education Research, highlighted in box 3.3, is a strong example of this type of coordinated effort.

A strong system of monitoring and evaluation not only provides information to improve policy design and facilitate the decisions policy makers need to take, but also serves as a base for the compilation and dissemination of the information students need to make education and career choices. This is the focus of the next section.

Disseminating Information to Help Students in Their Education and Career Choices

Jobs and careers are changing rapidly, with each day bringing expanded career opportunities in which choices are becoming harder to navigate. Career guidance is therefore both more important and more demanding for young students. If young people choose the wrong career, the costs of later changes can often be high. Therefore, providing adequate and easily accessible information to students to inform their choice of a technical or academic path and their selection of programs within either path is critical. Students may often choose a particular path based on familiarity, prestige, or informal guidance from family and friends. Although this is not always the cause of excess demand for certain educational paths or programs, misconceptions about returns to education, perceptions about prestige (particularly in the case of vocational and technical education), and lack of familiarity with different options can result in high demand for certain programs over others.

Individualized career guidance by professional career advisers in institutions such as schools is indispensable as students make these important decisions. Career advisers, when well trained as professionals, can provide critical information about labor markets and sources of additional information about specific careers. They are also able to draw out young people's aptitudes and interests to help them make realistic yet fulfilling choices. Career advisers, however, should be integrated within a comprehensive career guidance framework (OECD 2011)

Box 3.3   Australia's National Centre for Vocational Education Research

Australia's National Centre for Vocational Education Research (NCVER), established in 1981, conducts the systematized monitoring and evaluation that underpins VET policy. It is also recognized nationally and internationally as a leader in VET research. NCVER is a not-for-profit company owned by state, territory, and federal ministries. It is dependent on the Australian Department of Industry, which is responsible for skills development, research, and innovation policies. The Department of Industry provides 89 percent of NCVER revenues through contracts for management of the National VET Research Program and the Statistical Services Program. In 2012/13, this amounted to about $A $19.2 million. The rest of NCVER's revenues come mainly from commercial contracts.

Although NCVER is managed by a board of directors representing the state, territory, and Commonwealth governments, industry, unions, and training authorities, it functions as an independent body responsible for collecting, managing, analyzing, evaluating, and communicating research and statistics on VET. Some of its responsibilities are undertaking a strategic program of VET research, including the analytical services of the Longitudinal Surveys of Australian Youth (LSAY); collecting and analyzing national VET statistics and data; collecting and making available research findings on VET from around the world; disseminating the results of research and data analysis; and undertaking commercial consultancies where requested. NCVER's areas of data and research include student achievements and outcomes, career development, industry and employers (including skills shortages), VET-industry partnerships (including apprentices and trainees), research on the structure and performance of the VET system, and VET in the context of innovation, lifelong learning, and environmental and social issues, among other things.

The development of NCVER as a national strategy for VET research has had an important impact on the country. It provides major contributions to the formal knowledge base on VET in Australia and creates a robust national statistical evidence base to support M&E in Australia. It has also resulted in the development of a credible, highly skilled research community in VET in Australia. Much of this success has been the result of political continuity and ongoing support of NCVER throughout changing administrations at the national and subnational levels.

Sources: National Centre for Vocational Education Research; OECD 2009a.

---

that also includes easy-to-access information systems. Such system would include websites with career guidance or data on educational returns to allow students to make the most informed decisions possible. A stronger system of M&E that collects and processes systematic data is a first critical step, enabling students to make informed choices. A second step is making this information easily accessible to students and relevant stakeholders through websites. Countries that are moving in this direction include the United States, Chile, and Colombia.[5] Box 3.4 describes the experiences of Chile and the United States in developing such websites.

Some countries are taking a step further and offering intermediation services as students complete their degrees. These services fill important gaps and

Box 3.4 Information Systems: Examples from Chile and the United States

Experiences from Chile and the United States highlight how government-sponsored websites can provide prospective entrants to technical and higher education with highly reliable data on a variety of course-related information, including earnings for academic, technical, and vocational programs. The information generated by these systems may help mitigate the negative views of vocational and technical studies by simply presenting evidence of labor market outcomes for those who choose the vocational or technical tracks as opposed to some academic programs.

The *Occupational Outlook Handbook* (http://www.bls.gov/ooh/), housed in the U.S. Department of Labor's Bureau of Labor Statistics, provides career information on hundreds of occupations. The information is sorted by occupational group and searchable by median pay, minimum level of education for entry-level positions, type of on-the-job training and apprenticeships required, and the projected growth rate of the profession. A student can explore career and educational trajectories for occupations ranging from academic professions such as political science to the technical degrees needed by carpenters, information technology (IT) technicians, and surgical technicians, for example. The *Occupational Outlook Handbook* is one tool offered by the Bureau of Labor Statistics's larger website (http://www.bls.gov/), where a wide range of up-to-date data tools and publications are available to students, policy makers, and researchers.

Chile's site, "Mi Futuro"—My Future" (http://www.mifuturo.cl)—was created in 2006 by the higher education division of the Ministry of Education and grew out of Law 20.129 on Quality Assurance. This mandate requires the Ministry of Education to request, gather, and validate information, creating a national system of information. The system provides information for different types of higher education institutions, including universities, professional colleges, and technical colleges. The key indicators provided by the site are employability and earnings, but MiFuturo also gathers individual information and presents aggregate indicators and highly detailed information on enrollments, graduation rates, number of professors and instructors per institution, academic rates and financial aid, income, dispersion of income, and employability for different professional and technical careers. Because about 40 percent of students in tertiary education in Chile are enrolled in vocational or technical programs, MiFuturo provides valuable—and often difficult to process—information in an easily accessible format that helps students make more informed decisions when choosing between different options for tertiary and vocational and technical education.

Sources: MiFuturo, Ministry of Education, Government of Chile 2013, http://www.mifuturo.cl/; U.S. Bureau of Labor Statistics 2014.

---

may have a practical application for a VET system as well. For example, in Italy, the Alma Laurea consortium, offering systematic M&E at the university level, might be adaptable to technical education. Alma successfully integrates the collection of student data, labor market outcomes, and curricula vitae to provide the relevant stakeholders with a suite of services. These services integrate policy makers' needs for systematic, real-time data for policy-making decisions, employers' needs to hire qualified graduates, and students' needs for high-quality jobs and quick and effective insertion into the labor market. Box 3.5 provides more details on the Alma Laurea system.

Box 3.5 Alma Laurea, Italy: Placing Emphasis on Labor Market Intermediation

Alma Laurea is an interuniversity consortium that emerged in Italy in 1994 from the collaborative efforts of a group of researchers at the University of Bologna. They had set up a databank of students' curricula vitae (CVs) to aid in the evaluation of the role universities play in youth employability. Today, Alma Laurea is a consortium of 64 Italian universities, the Italian Ministry of Education, University and Research (MIUR), as well as companies and institutions that use Alma Laurea's databank and services. Alma Laurea has also signed agreements with other European universities. In Latin America and Asia, it facilitates the international labor market mobility of both Italian and foreign students in its networks.

Since 1994, Alma Laurea's portfolio of services has expanded from its start as a CV databank. Today, Alma Laurea offers a three-pillar approach to the provision of data, information, and career guidance to connect universities, students, and the labor market:

- *Graduates Profile*—an annual survey and report on the internal efficiency of the higher education system
- *Graduates' Employment Conditions*— an annual survey and report on the external efficiency of the higher education system
- *Online Databank of Graduates' Curricula Vitae*—a tool that improves the match between supply and demand of graduates and facilitates their transnational mobility. In Italy, the databank covers approximately 78 percent of Italian graduates and includes more than 1.72 million university-certified *curricula vitae*, which are translated into English.

Alma Laurea supplies the governing bodies of the consortium universities as well as the assessment units and committees dealing with teaching activities and career guidance with reliable data. Alma Laurea's data serve as a basis for national- and university-level policy making and activity planning, especially for the development and improvement of training activities and services that target students. Moreover, Alma Laurea creates more equal conditions for young people to access both the Italian and international labor markets. In 2007 an impact study of Alma Laurea concluded that graduates of universities in the consortium have more than a 2 percent higher chance of finding a job, have a 3 percent higher average monthly income, and are 2.5 percent more satisfied with their jobs (see Bagues and Labini 2009).

Sources: Alma Laurea; Bagues and Labini (2009).

Developing a Career Guidance Profession

In Brazil, individualized career guidance and the career guidance profession are incipient. Although school psychologists are often available in elite private schools to evaluate students' abilities or tendencies for certain vocations, outside of these schools such individualized guidance by trained psychologists is rare, making it a service often available only to the rich. Services available to the vast majority of students are few and far between.

Institutions such as the Sistema Nacional de Emprego (SINE, National Employment System) have local offices throughout the country. In addition to functioning as local employment offices, these offices provide matching and employment information services as well as administer unemployment insurance and other benefits. They also have counselors who advise those looking for employment. These counselors are usually not psychologists and are not typically professionals trained specifically in career guidance. Rather, they have a wide range of academic or professional profiles. At the moment, Brazil lacks a full-fledged national intervention to promote career guidance in which psychologists trained in career guidance are a key element. This has emerged as an important policy recommendation in the context of an expansion of VET nationwide.

Reviews of career guidance systems in the OECD have yielded some important observations to consider as Brazil continues to develop its own system as well as the career guidance profession. The first observation is the importance of career education and guidance in schools not only in helping young people to make the immediate choices that confront them but also in laying the foundation for lifelong learning and lifelong career development (Watts 2012). Career guidance should not only help students transition into the workplace, but also build the skills they need to manage their own careers over their lifetime. A second key observation is the risk of assimilating career counseling in schools in a holistic way that may include social, personal, and psychological counseling in addition to career counseling. The risk is that other, more immediate pressing needs may take up the counselor's time, marginalizing the role of career guidance (OECD 2011). Career counselors themselves should have good knowledge of labor markets, careers, and learning opportunities; an ability to identify additional relevant sources of information; and the training that gives them the set of competencies needed to help young people identify their interests and aptitudes and enable them to manage their own careers. To develop these types of professionals, Brazil will need stronger professional structures in the career guidance field as well as a competencies framework for the profession.

Box 3.6 highlights best practices in career study plans from the U.S. state of Virginia as one example of career guidance that starts even before students enter secondary education, allowing them to receive the information and resources needed to make an informed decision about a secondary education track (academic versus technical) and the tertiary education options and career tracks to which these choices can lead.

Box 3.6 Virginia's Academic and Career Plans of Study

Since 2006, the state of Virginia in the United States has developed a system of career clusters that organize academic and technical knowledge and skills into coherent sequences. The system aligns academic and technical skills with workplace readiness skills, and allows students, parents, and educators to identify pathways from secondary to postsecondary education. Moreover, the system of career clusters is based on the principle that different career pathways are made up of a set of knowledge and skills (both academic and technical) that give students a solid foundation, flexibility, and, later, a greater range of options.

Virginia's career clusters are also a key resource and organizing principle for school counselors, who use career clusters to help students explore their educational and career options. In the 2013/14 academic year, all schools began to develop a personal academic and career plan (ACP) for every student, starting with seventh graders (late primary education). These career plans are developed in a collaborative way by the student, the school counselor, and the student's parents or guardian; are based on the student's academic and career interests and a career assessment; and are aligned with a postsecondary career pathway or college entrance. The ACP suggests coursework through secondary education and points out examples of occupations in the given career pathway of interest to the student.

The ACP also becomes part of the student's academic record and so is passed on to the student's secondary education institution where it will be revised in the 9th and 11th grades. Virginia's ACPs are malleable plans intended to provide guidance to students in thinking about their career interests, but also to ensure that they are building a strong and adequate foundation in academic and technical subjects that will allow for transitions in and out of different career pathways and occupations later in life.

Source: Virginia Department of Education (2012), http://www.doe.virginia.gov/instruction/graduation/academic_career_plan/index.shtml.

Raising the Quality and Relevance of the VET System

Qualifications Frameworks and Certification: Increasing Transparency and Mobility

Most of the countries that have implemented a national qualifications framework (NQF) have done so for three reasons: (1) improving efficiency in the education sector and the labor market by reducing asymmetries of information, reducing transaction costs, and facilitating communication and transparency between both; (2) increasing the productivity and competitiveness of the country by facilitating and stimulating training; and (3) increasing the flexibility and mobility in both the education sector and the labor market by giving students and companies more information and options for education and training.

An NQF usually includes (1) a clear description of standards and competencies and skills for each level of the education and training system; (2) comparability of qualifications, whether certificate, diploma, or degree level; (3)

recognition of prior learning; (4) abolition of "dead end" courses to be replaced by a system of credits that enable individuals to continue to study at higher levels in the system; and, last but not least, (5) the contribution of a well-functioning and well-understood qualifications framework in enabling access and reentry for mature students, thereby strengthening the lifelong learning system.

Although Brazil does not have an NQF, it has taken smaller but important steps that build toward this end. As previously noted, Brazil's Rede: Certificação Profissional e Formação Inicial e Continuada (CERTIFIC, Network: Initial Training and Professional Certification and Continuation) certification is available in a wide variety of fields. It also has a national catalogue that lists the technical and professional education courses and programs available, together with the required minimum number of hours in each program. Nevertheless, beyond these efforts there is limited standardization of the skills and knowledge required of a person graduating from a particular technical program at a particular level (for example, a technical education qualification or degree in computer science). As a result, it is difficult for students to make informed choices about their education and training plans and for employers to ensure that a worker degree or other type of qualification in a particular field does in fact include the right competencies and skills to perform the required tasks. Similarly, education providers receive less guidance on how to structure curricula to ensure that students graduate with the most critical skills. As a long-term step, an NQF would provide a structure to simplify the qualifications system in an effort to increase understanding among all stakeholders. An NQF is usually based on levels, which are in turn based on standards of knowledge, skill, and competence, and incorporates awards made for all kinds of learning, wherever it is gained. Qualifications achieved in school, further education and training, and higher education and training are usually all included.

Establishing consistent standards in education and training, promoting quality, and increasing access, transfer, and progression opportunities for learners and the ability to understand and compare qualifications at home and abroad (that is, qualifications recognition) are the cornerstone of the NQF. All of these issues are central to the learner and, as a consequence, are of fundamental importance to those providing advice to learners.

Many policy makers cite the potential benefits of a well-organized, widely accepted national qualifications framework. However, it is also important to keep in mind some of the risks involved in centralizing qualification and certification systems at the national level. International experience has revealed that certification systems generally require a high administrative capacity to establish and effectively manage such a system, as well as strong buy-in from parents, teachers, students, and other stakeholders (Botero 2013). Such a system is also very costly. These factors present additional challenges for a large and diverse country like Brazil. Although such a framework may eventually be an ambitious goal for Brazil, in the meantime it can take further steps to foster collaboration and partnerships between stakeholders in order to map the skills and competencies required of certain occupations and ensure that educational providers are producing graduates with these levels and types of skills.

Many countries such as Australia, Germany, Mexico, New Zealand, and South Africa have opted to develop an NQF. Mexico's Occupational Competency Standardization and Certification Council (CONOCER) is one example of the importance of developing a skills certification system and qualifications framework (see box 3.7). CONOCER standardizes the competencies required of occupations (as a basis for skills certification) to better align VET curricula with the labor market while increasing the social and economic value of VET. The system ultimately aims to improve the competitiveness and productivity of different economic sectors of the country. Although CONOCER has suffered setbacks and slow development over the last decade, Mexico is currently the only country in the region with an NQF, and it could provide insight and lessons for Brazil.

Improving Teacher Preparedness

Anecdotal evidence suggests that the difficulties in finding and hiring well-trained teachers with relevant experience for teaching VET hamper the ability of institutions to manage the most adequate portfolio of courses that would meet

---

Box 3.7 Mexico's Occupational Competency Standardization and Certification Council (CONOCER)

CONOCER is a semistate entity administered by Mexico's secretary of public education. The objective is to develop and promote competencies models in order to increase competitiveness and productivity throughout the Mexican economy. CONOCER is responsible for ensuring continuous education and skill development of labor in Mexico and for promoting a culture of competency-based certification throughout the country. More specifically, CONOCER improves the quality of firms, workers, and training providers by defining standards for the development of labor competency qualifications and ensuring that these qualifications are based on the needs and requirements of firms. This process originates with a series of competency committees, supported by groups of technical experts from each sector, who orient the development of competency standards. This process grew out of the recent restructuring CONOCER that put it in a lead role in a process of dialogues with industry and economic sector leaders and stakeholders in order to gain insight into the needs of these sectors. This process functions as a first critical step toward aligning VET curricula to the needs of the labor market in different parts of the country and improving the competitiveness of each sector. The competencies model stands to increase the social recognition and esteem of students and workers for VET and to make it a more attractive educational option as well as increase the economic value of VET for industry in Mexico.

Sources: OECD 2009b; CONOCER, http://www.conocer.gob.mx/.

the labor market needs in Brazil. Interviews with counterparts in Brazil have revealed that private providers in the Brazilian VET system seem to be better placed to adapt their courses to the market needs, including reacting to seasonal demands. This adaptability is mainly a result of private providers' autonomy and ability to make changes in teaching staff. Nevertheless, with the exception of Sistema S, these private providers consistently attract less prepared and thus less effective teachers. Public providers, by contrast, are able to attract better candidates to VET, but job stability leaves little room for permeability between teaching and working in industry and other sectors and does little to give teachers incentives to keep their skills up to date. It also creates something of a lag in keeping course offerings current with the evolving needs of different sectors—especially specific classes within VET programs that teach cutting-edge technologies in that field—because of the strict policies on the hiring, firing, and reallocation of teachers that restrain the flexibility needed to create or eliminate different course offerings.

One of the main challenges internationally, as well as for expansion of the federal- and state-level technical schools in Brazil, is to find the right set of teachers who combine both academic and practical, hands-on knowledge. It is well known that a key feature of successful VET programs is that courses are taught by teachers and trainers who are both well prepared and well acquainted with the needs of modern industry—and more innovative. In Brazil, regulations usually require that VET teachers at the tertiary level be proficient in academic publications and research, which is not necessarily appropriate for a VET teacher. In most VET fields, a teacher or industry professional turned teacher should be someone with experience in developing new products, processes, and technologies. A patent under a teacher's belt might produce a more relevant and valuable perspective for teaching VET than a PhD, depending on the subject matter. Experiences from several OECD countries have revealed that teachers and trainers should be encouraged to spend some of their time working in industry, and VET systems should promote flexible pathways of recruitment to make it easier for those with industry skills to become part of the workforce in VET institutions. VET systems also should provide the appropriate pedagogical training for trainers and supervisors of interns, trainees, and apprentices in workplaces and adapt the level of preparation to the nature of the workplace learning being provided. Interchange and partnership between VET institutions and sectors should be encouraged so that vocational teachers and trainers spend time in industry to update their knowledge. Similarly, vocational trainers in firms should spend some time in VET institutions to enhance their pedagogical skills.

In addition to the uneven quality of the private provision of VET in Brazil, the relevance of state-run technical and vocational training may be less than optimal because of several factors, not least of these being faculty who quickly grow out of touch with the constantly evolving needs of the labor market.[6]

Some states such as Ceará have been successful in implementing programs in collaboration with other institutions to build their workforce of VET teachers and trainers. Box 3.8 describes the state's efforts to find a middle ground between offering an attractive package that lures better-quality teachers while maintaining flexibility.

The Swiss model of teacher training is another example of successful teacher training resulting in a well-prepared yet flexible VET teaching force. Box 3.9 describes this system in more detail. For Brazil, a medium- and long-term strategy for the development of trainers and instructors may be needed to ensure that the supply of high-quality, well-prepared VET teachers continues to grow in step with demand.

Box 3.8 Building a Flexible Cadre of Teachers

The government of Ceará is an example of the potential for innovation in the provision of VET. The state introduced a level of flexibility into its VET system that is atypical in Brazil for publicly provided VET. In 1998 Ceará began offering state-provided VET for the first time. However, the state opted to leverage federal and federal resources to establish the Centro de Educação Tecnológica (CENTEC, Center for Technological Education, a nongovernmental organization—NGO, organização social) which was created to partner with the state government for the provision of VET.

Under Brazilian law, there are several advantages to having an NGO provide VET in Ceará, most notably the flexibility in hiring teachers. This flexibility stands in stark contrast to the experience of public VET providers. CENTEC can hire, reallocate, and dismiss teachers in accordance with local needs and for specific types of VET programs. For example, teachers can be easily allocated to another function or another program in a different area of the state as needed. For CENTEC, it is easier to create and eliminate VET programs or specific courses as local demand changes. Public VET providers usually can only offer a temporary program of courses for a limited range of subjects because they are restricted to using the available teachers. This limits the range of expertise available for staffing different kinds of vocational and technical programs and course offerings as needs evolve.

Although CENTEC provides technical programs in the concomitante and subsequente modalities, also frequently provides teachers for technical courses in the integrado modality. In Ceará, these courses have a compulsory apprenticeship component, which requires that an adviser be assigned to support students in apprenticeships. Many teachers execute both functions—teacher and adviser—because each one is a half-year commitment. This allows part-time teachers to remain employed year-round. Offering this kind of arrangement to public providers would require changes to the laws governing public teacher benefits and job stability—a step that is not necessary when CENTEC hires teachers.

Source: Secretary of education, Ceará, 2012.

Box 3.9 VET Teacher and Trainer Preparedness in Switzerland

Among the many strengths of the Swiss VET system is the preparedness of its teachers and trainers. They are both well prepared in their particular discipline as well as trained in VET-specific pedagogies. Teachers and trainers are required to have a professional college degree (a higher education degree or an equivalent qualification in their chosen field), and both full- and part-time teachers are required to pursue an additional vocational pedagogy program that averages 300 hours. This additional program is particularly important for teachers of general subjects (such as physics for engineers) so that they can tailor these subjects to the needs of VET students. VET teacher preparation is carried out and coordinated by the Swiss Federal Institute for Vocational Training and Education, which also offers continuing education to upgrade current teachers' skills and conducts evaluations and research to help guide VET-focused policy making.

VET teaching is also considered highly prestigious in Switzerland, and a high degree of flexibility is integrated into the profession, making it both more attractive as a profession to potential VET teachers and trainers as well as more effective. Part-time teaching arrangements in Switzerland allow teachers to maintain jobs in their respective industries, lessening the trade-off between choosing a career in industry where salaries remain more competitive over a position in teaching. At the same, this flexibility between positions in industry and teaching ensures that teachers stay current with the skills and knowledge needed in a rapidly changing modern economy and are able to develop their own curricula within the certified curricula of their institutions.

Sources: Fazekasm and Field 2013; OECD 2011.

Promoting Innovation in VET

In a recent study of firm innovation, Latin America ranked poorly. Lederman et al. (2013) report that in Latin America firms introduce new products less frequently than firms in otherwise similar economies; high-end entrepreneurs tend to be far from adapting global best practices in the management of their enterprises; firms' investment in R&D is low; and patent activity is well below benchmark levels. In order to grow or even survive, firms need to continually innovate. In this domain of entrepreneurship, businesses in Latin America score relatively badly. Some of the most successful firms in Latin America and the Caribbean managed to grow out of their national boundaries during the last decade and are now competing in world markets. However, the success of high-end companies such as Vale, Embraer, and CEMEX notwithstanding, innovation in Latin America is limited, with even some of the giant *multilatinas* underperforming their peers from other countries. Many formal firms in the region are engaged in some form of innovation, but the intensity of innovation tends to be low or poorly suited to raising productivity. Human capital, particularly the comparatively low number of engineers and scientists produced in the region, is one of the explanatory factors for low levels of innovation and productivity in the region, including in Brazil (Lederman et al. 2013).

In this context, Brazil should consider promoting a system of VET that not only addresses the expansion of skilled labor, but also promotes innovation and competitiveness at the firm level. This is one way to improve levels of productivity that have remained somewhat stagnant and continue to hinder further growth. Although Brazil may need active policies to increase the number of specific occupations produced by the education system, especially at the tertiary and postgraduate levels (such as engineers and scientists), this report suggests two possible classroom interventions to help the VET system become more innovative and therefore develop more innovative students at the upper secondary level of education and beyond. It also presents one system intervention, drawing on the example of community colleges in the U.S. city of Chicago, that can help focus changes in pedagogy and curricula in a way that can help Brazilian firms become more innovative and stay on the frontier of knowledge.

Brazil at High Speed: Innovation in a Diverse Environment

Many of the recommendations in this report are focused on making the existing institutional structure function more efficiently and effectively. In a country of many growth "speeds," however, some regions may be still be in the process of strengthening the institutional structures that contribute to and govern technical and vocational education, whereas others are more mature and better placed to compete on a global frontier of innovation and knowledge. As noted, the shortage of engineers may potentially be a constraint for sectors of the Brazilian economy that could potentially be at the forefront of the knowledge frontier. In Chicago, the community college system has been revamped to carefully consider these types of strategic industries and the ways in which VET can contribute to competitiveness (see box 3.10).

Innovation in the VET Classroom

Refocusing VET pedagogies on solving the real-world challenges presented by companies is one way of ensuring that students are applying their learning in a way that will be required in the workplace. This may also be one way to help address the lack of apprenticeship opportunities available to all VET students. At the same time, technical education must incorporate the latest technology and offer a set of physical tools so that students can have the space to apply their learning in new and innovative ways. Building the infrastructure and supplying every VET institution with the technology available in economic sectors is both costly and unrealistic, especially in the most remote regions of

Box 3.10 VET for Innovation and Competitiveness: Chicago's City Colleges

Launched in 2011, Chicago's Career to College (C2C) program is embedded in an ambitious effort to overhaul the city's network of seven public city colleges (community colleges). The program currently serves 115,000 students, many from disadvantaged backgrounds. Christened "Reinvention," the reform aims to position the City Colleges of Chicago (CCC) as a key instrument in simultaneously solving two present-day problems: (1) raising workforce skills to meet the skills gaps (particularly in the most critical global industries) that Chicago's employers face and (2) increasing the colleges' ability to offer both "access and success" to the city's youth and adults.

The C2C program targets economic sectors in the Chicago area with strong growth prospects over the next decade, including health care; transportation, distribution, and logistics; hospitality and the culinary arts; high-tech manufacturing; information technology; and business and professional services. Each of the colleges works with employers in one of these economic sectors, effectively becoming a center of excellence for that sector. The strategic goal of C2C is to have each college co-design with employer's job-relevant curricula for their designated sector. These redesigned curricula and pedagogical practices can then serve as a template for improving teaching and learning throughout the CCC system. A key feature of the new curricula is stackable credentials that are intended to expand learning pathways to jobs for youth, as well as for adults who need the skills to start new careers or progress in their current one.

An impressive array of employers—more than 100 to date—participate in multiple roles: (1) as providers of labor market information; (2) as providers of information on occupational standards; (3) as collaborators with faculty in creating new curricula, in validating or fine-tuning existing programs, and in defining program sequencing and learning pathways through the device of "stackable credentials;" (4) as guides in the identification of industry certificates with high economic value (5) as hosts of internships for students and faculty; (6) as sources of practitioner-experts to co-teach C2C courses; and (7) as customers of C2C training programs for their workers. These multiple roles strengthen employers' voices in the C2C initiative and enable it to benefit from timely advice to enhance the market relevance of C2C.

Three elements are especially important: (1) the sustainability of employers' involvement; (2) private sector experience; and (3) globalization and the pressure on firms to upgrade skills as a part of their strategy for competitiveness. Moreover, C2C's industry partners have all committed to giving graduates of the C2C programs job interviews!

Source: World Bank 2013.

Brazil. Nevertheless, innovative models of relatively low-cost, multipurpose, and yet high-tech laboratories such as the fab labs model developed by the Massachusetts Institute of Technology (MIT) or similar "maker spaces" could be one way of giving students the tools to innovate both inside and outside the classroom (see box 3.11).

Box 3.11 Ideas for Innovating in VET

Tools for innovation. Fab labs, short for fabrication laboratories, began as an outreach project in MIT's Center for Bits and Atoms (CBA). They were devised to give the public access to design and manufacturing tools previously available only to engineers at big companies or large research universities. By contrast, thes smaller workshops typically need little more than a large room and are relatively cheap to set up (US$50,000–100,000). They consist of high-tech but versatile and easy to learn technologies and tools that allow the user to build a prototype of "almost anything." These types of laboratories are often complemented by classes that employ innovative methodologies and project-based learning to teach users to turn their ideas into products and apply them to solving local problems. Models of these types of lab have cropped up in different parts of the world and have been used to create solutions that range from simple household needs such as wi-fi antennas or sensors to warn that a cow has strayed into the family garden, to more complex solar- and wind-powered turbines and analytical instruments for agriculture and health care and other industries. Most recently, fab labs and similar models of low-cost, high-tech, and easy to use laboratories are increasingly being linked to institutions that provide vocational and technical education at both the secondary and tertiary levels, particularly in the United States. Many of these labs are integrated into technical education curricula, and teachers build time in these laboratories into their lesson plans. The labs provide students with an opportunity for hands-on experience, allowing them to develop an innovative and entrepreneurial mindset, in addition to strong technical skills, that is applicable to industries that range from hairdressing to renewable energy and facilitate lifelong learning

Pedagogies for innovation. Case study-based learning and other pedagogies and curricula that promote learning through real-world challenges are another way to develop innovative students in VET. In the United Kingdom, for example, several vocational and technical schools are using case studies of real-world challenges as a way to teach VET curricula. Focused on these challenges, students are able to benefit from hands-on experience in directly applying the concepts they are learning in the classroom in a way that will be required of them in the workplace. Moreover, students are also creating solutions to existing problems using the skills they are learning—an arrangement that promotes innovation and an entrepreneurship mindset that students will take into the workplace. Similarly, students can enter into student competitions with the solutions they present, providing an additional incentive for them and giving greater recognition and prestige to vocational and technical education.

Sources: Center for Bits and Atoms, MIT, http://cba.mit.edu/; Fuller and Unwin 2012.

Implications for PRONATEC: Expanding VET and Reaching the Most Vulnerable

The expansion of VET under the Programa Nacional de Acesso ao Ensino Técnico e Emprego (PRONATEC, National Program for Access to Technical Education and Employment) raises the questions of whether the program is bringing the low-income students and vulnerable populations targeted by PRONATEC on board and what the returns to this investment for this group really are. Even though all five strategic points discussed in this chapter have immediate implications for PRONATEC, establishing and consolidating a solid M&E system for the successful and sustainable implementation of PRONATEC is especially important. For example, PRONATEC's evolution is regularly monitored by Brazil's Ministério da Educação (MEC, Ministry of Education) through the Sistema Nacional de Informações da Educação Profissional e Tecnológica (SISTEC, National System of Professional and Technological Education), including the Free of Charge VET Vacancies Agreement between MEC and Sistema S. Through SISTEC, MEC conducts a federal monitoring system that collects information on a range of student socioeconomic characteristics for all students who have completed or are completing technical courses at the upper secondary level. To date, however, the system only gathers information on students in cursos de formação inicial e continuada (FICs, initial and continuing training courses) when they are provided by institutions that also offer technical courses. This is problematic, however, because a substantial part of PRONATEC is focused on expanding and improving FIC courses, which are not necessarily covered by SISTEC. Finally, because SISTEC is used as well to monitor the agreement between MEC and Sistema S on free of charge VET vacancies, it also lacks the more complete set of data that could help to better monitor resource allocation under this agreement.

In addition to the five strategic points previously discussed, this section describes three strategic issues on which policy makers should focus to ensure PRONATEC's success.

First, technical education in Brazil is still (perhaps inadvertently) targeting students from a relatively high socioeconomic level. Clearly, there is a need to rethink the contents and overall course load in technical education not only to make courses more attractive to the labor market but also to students considering the technical track.[7] Table 3.2 reports the mandatory classroom hours for the upper secondary education, academic, and technical tracks. Students in the academic upper secondary track complete 2,400 hours or approximately 800 hours

Table 3.2 Secondary Education Course Loads, Total Hours per Year by Modality: Brazil, 2012

Modality of upper secondary education	Academic course load	Technical course load[a]	Total
Concomitante	2,400	800–1,200	3,200–3,600
Subsequente	2,400	800–1,200	3,200–3,600
Integrado	2,200	800–1,200	3,000–3,400
Academic	2,400	n.a.	2,400

Source: Based on Resolução No. 1, Conselho Nacional de Educação (CNE, National Council of Education).
Note: n.a. = not applicable.
a. Course load excludes additional hours for completion of apprenticeships.

per year. By contrast, students completing technical education in the concomitante and subsequente modalities complete the entire course load for academic upper secondary, plus the minimum course load for their chosen field of technical education. Technical education programs usually consume between 800 and 1,200 hours per year (for more complex programs). This represents between 266 and 400 more hours per year than the number of hours of peers completing only the academic track. Students in the integrado modality, however, reduce their academic subjects to complete their technical education course load, resulting in a savings of about 200–400 hours over the course of their upper secondary education as compared with students in the first two modalities. None of these legally mandated course loads includes additional hours for apprenticeships, which may need to be completed in addition to the mandatory classroom hours.

Schwartzman (2014) notes that while an optimistic hypothesis is that students taking technical education in the two first modalities are building a stronger and broader set of skills, the more realistic hypothesis is that academic secondary education courses are perceived as a bureaucratic requirement. The additional course load in the concomitante and subsequente modes compared with the integrado mode also represents a higher cost in terms of time and effort that may not be warranted. Students in the more selective *integrado* modality tend to be those who are already stronger students with plans to continue on to tertiary education.

Almeida et al. (2015) both complement and confirm this hypothesis. Their research on the returns to technical education profiles the students who most commonly frequent each modality of technical education. They find that in recent years students in all technical tracks come from a higher socioeconomic background (higher per capita income) than the average comparable student in academic secondary education. Figure 3.1 illustrates this fact for the different modalities of education.

Figure 3.1 Percentage of Students by Type of Course and Income Quintile: Brazil, 2007

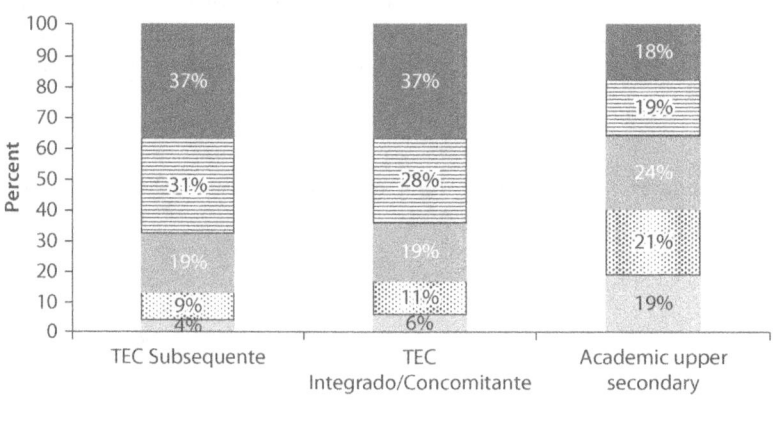

Source: Based on Almeida et al. (2015).
Note: TEC = technical education.

Figure 3.2 Wage Premiums for Technical Education Graduates Relative to Those with Only Academic Upper-Secondary Education, 2007

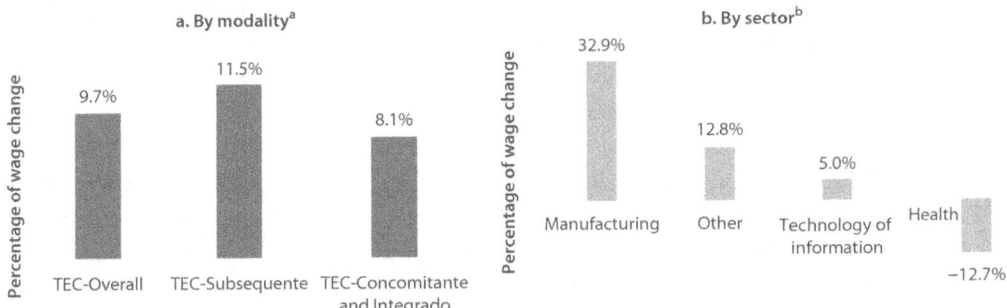

Source: Almeida et al. (2015) based on PNAD (2007).
Note: Figure reports the propensity score matching estimates of the wage premiums for graduates in the technical track at the upper-secondary level using data from IBGE (2007). TEC = ensino técnico (technical education)
a. "TEC Subsequente" is a technical program for students who have already concluded an academic upper-secondary program. "TEC Integrado" includes academic and vocational courses offered as one program in the same school. "TEC Concomitante" is a complementary, but separate, technical program for students who are completing an academic upper-secondary program, frequently carried out in two separate schools. Graph reports the returns depending by type of training modality: Overall (including all modalities), subsequente, or comcomitante. "TEC-Overall" graduates (including concomitante, subsequente, and integrado) averaged a 9.7 percent higher hourly wage than graduates of the general upper-secondary academic track. Similarly, TEC-Subsequente graduates averaged an 11.5 percent higher hourly wage. TEC-Concomitante and TEC-Integrado graduates averaged an 8.1 percent higher hourly wage.
b. The graph reports overall wage returns for technical education graduates relative to general academic upper-secondary graduates by the sector of current activity. "Other" includes other courses that are not classified as manufacturing, technology of information, management, agriculture or health.

Almeida et al. (2015) also find that students that completed technical education at the upper secondary level have higher wage returns—a premium of approximately 9.7 percent to their education than comparable students with only a secondary academic education. Figure 3.2 reports these results for across different modalities and sectors.

These findings have two important policy implications for PRONATEC. The first is that returns to technical education tend to be higher in the northeast of Brazil where the provision of VET is smaller, and, second, that returns tend to be higher for technical education in the fields of industry and informatics.

The second issue is that more research is needed on how PRONATEC will affect the employment and earnings opportunities for the most vulnerable. Because PRONATEC is investing heavily in this expansion through Bolsa Formação Estudante (Scholarship for Student Training) via the concomitante modality, there is a clear opportunity for further evaluation and research. Bolsa Formação (Scholarship for Student Training) targets low-income students and low-skilled workers and finances technical courses for students in public network and FIC courses for beneficiaries of unemployment insurance and social assistance programs.[8] In particular, it is important to evaluate whether PRONATEC is actually reaching this target population and whether these courses are having an impact on the labor market outcomes of students. This is especially important because of the historical tendency for technical education students overall to be relatively better off than their peers in the academic secondary tracks. Challenges such as having to complete a heavier course load in the concomitante modality or the opportunity cost in terms of the time, effort, and resources needed to complete an additional secondary technical degree in the subsequente modality (typically completed in evening classes, which generally are of lower quality) may prove a much higher barrier for lower-income students.

Third, with the expansion of PRONATEC there is room to conduct rigorous impact evaluations to assess the cost-effectiveness of many of the programs as well as the most effective ways of delivering them. This has already been done for several other policy questions in Brazil. In particular, the answers to two very important questions are of critical importance for the successful implementation of VET policies and of PRONATEC. The first concerns constructing more and better evidence on labor market returns to technical education vis-á-vis the general secondary education track. The second concerns second-generation questions on how these programs should be delivered on the ground. How effective are on-the-job components versus more academic learning? How important is it to complement cognitive learning with noncognitive life skills for some of the groups? How effective is a system of career guidance in promoting the integration of students into the labor market? For one particular policy, there may be room for an impact evaluation based on a pilot: the evaluation of how well at-distance learning for VET students (E-TEC Brasil) produces high-quality graduates with the skills needed by the labor market. This is especially relevant to the poorest states and the most remote locations where it is challenging to recruit high-quality teachers and to provide students with more diverse VET programs when the job market for some skills is not strong.

Notes

1. This approach is not new. In other countries, employers have organized themselves into self-selected sector skills councils. This allows them to organize their demand for skills by taking a lead role in managing their relationship with the government, the schools, and the trainees. The key ingredient in this relationship is employer-defined occupational standards, which determine how training providers organize their programs as well as the benchmarks against which trainees are certified.
2. Through a joint program with local industry, technical education graduates in Ceará take advantage of six-month internships at a state-subsidized wage. After the internship, a graduate may opt to stay in the workforce or move on to higher education. Bruns, Evans, and Luque (2012) describe Ceará's schools as best practice in the OECD. The schools ensure that students at all points in their education are qualified to move back and forth from the labor force to the formal schooling system. This is especially important because a problem with many vocationally oriented schooling in several parts of the world has been the low academic content, leaving students unprepared for further formal education.
3. http://www.empresas.ciee.org.br.
4. For a discussion see Almeida, Behrman, and Robalino (2011).

5. SINES (Sistema Nacional de Informacion de Educacion Superior, National Information System for Higher Education) is the basis for Graduados Colombia, a labor market observatory that provides students, graduates, higher education institutions, researchers, and the private sector with links to job offers, advice on creating a curriculum vita, salaries, financing options for education, and studies on different economic sectors (http://www.mineducacion.gov.co/snies).

6. Bruns, Evans, and Luque (2012) identify several factors that account for the often poor quality of state-level technical education. They contend that courses are often relatively expensive because they re-create industrial equipment in a school setting and yet are of low quality because both the equipment and faculty quickly grow out of touch with the labor market. The state of Minas Gerais, according to Bruns, Evans, and Luque, appears to have found a creative and pragmatic way to avoid these problems by combining the relative strengths of the public sector (accreditation, quality assurance, and funding equalization) and the private sector (labor market relevance and flexibility). Further details on the VET system in Minas Gerais can be found in box 2.2 in chapter 2.

7. As figure 1.6 illustrates, in Brazil the majority of VET students enroll in technical education in the subsequente modality, after they have completed secondary education, or in the concomitante modality, as a second set of coursework in the evenings or afternoons after their academic secondary classes. Only about 21 percent of technical education students study in the integrado modality, which represents a lower overall course load integrating both technical and academic subjects in a full day of class.

8. Bolsa-Formação offers free places in professional and technological education. It has two modes: Bolsa Formação, which offers initial and continuing courses (short courses, with 160 class hours or more) to beneficiaries of unemployment insurance and productive inclusion programs of the federal government, and Bolsa Formação Estudante, which offers technical courses (longer duration, at least 800 classroom hours) for students in the public networks.

References

Almeida, Rita, Jere Behrman, and David Robalino, eds. 2011. *The Right Skills for the Job? Rethinking Training Policies for Workers*. Washington, DC: World Bank.

Almeida, Rita Kullberg, Leandro Anazawa, Naercio Menezes Filho, and Ligia Maria De Vasconcellos. 2015. "Investing in Technical & Vocational Education and Training: Does It Yield Large Economic Returns in Brazil." Policy Research Working Paper no. WPS 7246, World Bank Group, Washington, D.C. http://documents.worldbank.org/curated/en/2015/04/24411547/investing-technical-vocational-education-training-yield-large-economic-returns-brazil.

Araneda, Hernan. 2013. *Mining Workforce Planning and Development in Chile: Towards a Sectorial Skills Strategy*. Santiago: Fundacion Chile.

Bagues, Manuel F., and Mauro Sylos Labini. 2009. "Do Online Labor Market Intermediaries Matter? The Impact of Alma Laurea on the University-to-Work Transition." In *Studies of Labor Market Intermediation*. Chicago: University of Chicago Press.

Botero, Javier. 2013. *Propuestas de Ajustes a Documentos Tecnicos y de Institucionalidad y Gobernanza de un Marco nacional de Cualificaiones*. Bogotá: Departamento Nacional de Planeación.

Bruns, Barbara, David Evans, and Javier Luque. 2012. *Achieving World-Class Education in Brazil: The Next Agenda*. Washington, DC: World Bank.

Fazekasm, Mihaly and Simon Field. 2013. *Skills beyond School: Review of Switzerland*. Paris: Organisation for Economic Co-operation and Development.

Ferraz, Claudioa and a and Barbara Bruns. 2012. "Paying Teachers to Perform: The Impact of Bonus Pay in Pernambuco, Brazil." *Society for Research on Educational Effectiveness*.

Fuller, Alison and Lorna Unwin. 2012. "What's the Point of Adult Apprenticeships?" *Adults Learning* 23 (3): 8–13.

IBGE (Instituto Brasileiro de Geografia e Estatistica/Brazilian Insitute for Geography and Statistics). 2007. Contagem da Populacao, Brazil.

ILO-EFT-UNESCO (International Labour Organization, European Training Foundation, and United Nations Educational, Scientific and Cultural Organization). 2012. "Proposed Indicators for Assessing Technical and Vocational Education and Training Inter-Agency Working Group on TVET Indicators." April. http://www.etf.europa.eu/webatt.nsf/0/E112211E42995263C12579EA002EF821/$file/Report%20on%20indicators%20April%202012.pdf .

Kemple, James J. 2008. *Career Academics: Long-Term Impacts on Labor Market Outcomes, Education Attainment, and Transitions to Adulthood*. New York: MDRC.

Kuczera, Malgorzata, Giorgio Brunello, Simon Field, and Nancy Hoffman. 2008. *Learning for Jobs: OECD Reviews of Vocational Education and Training: Norway*. Paris: Organisation for Economic Co-operation and Development.

Lederman, Daniel, Julian Messina, Samuel Pienknagura, and Jamele Rigolini. 2013. *Latin American Entrepreneurs: Many Firms but Little Innovation*. Washington, DC: World Bank.

Nam, Yoo Jeung Joy. 2009. "Pre-Employment Skills Development Strategies in the OECD." Social Protection and Labor Unit, World Bank, Washington, DC.

Neri, Marcelo. 2010. "A Educação Profissional e Você no Mercado de Trabalho." Fundacao Getulio Vargas.

OECD (Organisation for Economic Co-operation and Development). 2009a. "OECD/CERI Study of Systemic Innovation in VET: Systemic Innovation in the Australian VET System: Country Case Study Report." http://www.oecd.org/australia/42243354.pdf.

———. 2009b. "OECD/CERI Study of Systemic Innovation in VET: Systemic Innovation in the Mexican VET System: Country Case Study Report." http://www.oecd.org/mexico/43139985.pdf.

———. 2010. "Good Practices in TVET Reform." http://unesdoc.unesco.org/images/0018/001870/187038e.pdf.

———. 2011. "Learning for Jobs: Pointers for Policy Development: OECD Reviews of Vocational Education and Training." Directorate for Education, Education and Training Policy Division. http://www.oecd.org/edu/skills-beyond-school/48078260.pdf.

———. 2013. *Skills Development and Training in SMEs, Local Economic and Employment Development (LEED)*. Paris: OECD Publishing. http://dx.doi.org/10.1787/9789264169425-en.

PNAD (Pesquisa Nacional por Amostra de Domicílios/National Household Sample Survey). 2007. IBGE (Instituto Brasileiro de Geografia e Estatistica/Brazilian Insitute for Geography and Statistics), Brazil.

Schwartzman, S. 2014. "Academic Drift in Brazilian Education." In The Forefront of International Higher Education, 61-72. Netherlands: Springer Science and Business Media.

SEDUC (Secretaria da Educação, Governo do Estado do Ceará/Department of Education, State of Ceara). 2012. Brazil. http://www.seduc.ce.gov.br/.

Stach, Walter, and Gabriele Stoger. 2009. "European Year of Creativity and Innovation: Exploration and Analysis of 'Creativity and Innovation in Initial Vocational Education and Training' Based on Experience Gained from 7 EU Member States and 12 Apprenticeship Trades." Paper commissioned by the Federal Ministry for Education, the Arts and Culture, Austria.

Vasconcellos, Lígia, Fernanda Costa Lima, Julia Guerra Fernandes, and Naercio Menezes-Filho. 2010. "Avaliação Econômica Do Ensino Médio Profissional." Fundação Itaú Social, Brasilia.

Virginia Department of Education. 2012. "Graduation Requirements: Academic and Career Plan." http://www.doe.virginia.gov/instruction/graduation/academic_career_plan/index.shtml.

Watts, A. G. 2012. *Policy and Practice in Career Guidance: An International Perspective*. Paris: Organization for Economic Co-operation and Development. http://www.oecd.org/edu/innovation-education/1963023.pdf.

World Bank. 2013. "Background on Chicago's College-to-Careers Program: Reflections from a Learning Journey during April 23–24, 2013." World Bank Learning Journey, April 23–24, 2013. http://siteresources.worldbank.org/EDUCATION/Resources/278200-1121703274255/1439264-1380745447281/Background_Learning_Journey_9_2.pdf.

CHAPTER 4

Policy Directions for Reform

Summary

Although Brazil has made significant progress in education over the last decades in expanding both access and quality, significant challenges remain. Low completion rates at the upper secondary level and poor quality of learning are still striking facts. As of 2010, 19 percent of Brazil's 15- to 24-year-olds were neither in school nor working. For this population, opportunities in the labor market are reduced and of poor quality. In addition, anecdotal evidence suggests that Brazilian firms face skills gaps or mismatches that constrain labor productivity and firm growth, including in certain technical and socioemotional skills. Brazil is now massively investing in a scale-up of vocational and technical education and training (VET) through the national flagship program, Programa Nacional de Acesso ao Ensino Técnico e Emprego (PRONATEC, National Program for Access to Technical Education and Employment), and this report represents the first comprehensive mapping of VET institutions and policies in the country. The report shares international best practices on the operational issues identified as critical bottlenecks in the delivery of technical education. It also draws on interviews with federal- and state-level clients and counterparts, including inputs provided by the Ministério da Educação (Ministry of Education), and a desk review of existing work in order to take a critical and in-depth look at strategic institutional and policy issues.

The findings reveal that because of the diversity and complexity in the delivery of VET in Brazil, it is not possible to have a one-size-fits-all solution to improving the delivery of technical education across states and providers. However, five strategic priorities are critical for nationwide improvements in the delivery of VET in Brazil:

1. Align the provision of technical education with the needs of the labor market, including cognitive and socioemotional skills.
2. Implement a robust monitoring and evaluation system, placing special emphasis on tracking learning and labor market outcomes.

3. Develop a career guidance framework to support students in their education and professional career decisions.
4. Promote teacher preparedness for a more "relevant" technical education.
5. Promote more innovative pedagogical practices and cost-effective infrastructure.

The report concludes with a discussion of the main implications for the implementation of PRONATEC in the years ahead. In addition to the five strategic priorities, this report emphasizes the importance of taking advantage of this rapid scale-up of PRONATEC to ensure that pilots are well evaluated, especially their impact on labor market outcomes and productivity for different target groups.

ECO-AUDIT

Environmental Benefits Statement

The World Bank Group is committed to reducing its environmental footprint. In support of this commitment, the Publishing and Knowledge Division leverages electronic publishing options and print-on-demand technology, which is located in regional hubs worldwide. Together, these initiatives enable print runs to be lowered and shipping distances decreased, resulting in reduced paper consumption, chemical use, greenhouse gas emissions, and waste.

The Publishing and Knowledge Division follows the recommended standards for paper use set by the Green Press Initiative. The majority of our books are printed on Forest Stewardship Council (FSC)–certified paper, with nearly all containing 50–100 percent recycled content. The recycled fiber in our book paper is either unbleached or bleached using totally chlorine free (TCF), processed chlorine free (PCF), or enhanced elemental chlorine free (EECF) processes.

More information about the Bank's environmental philosophy can be found at http://crinfo.worldbank.org/wbcrinfo/node/4.

www.ingramcontent.com/pod-product-compliance
Lightning Source LLC
Chambersburg PA
CBHW082127230426
43671CB00015B/2831